TECHNIQUES FOR MANAGING A SAFE SCHOOL

Beverley **H.** *Johns*

Four Rivers Special Education District, Jacksonville, Illinois

John **P.** *Keenan*

Assistant Chief of Police, Jacksonville, Illinois

LOVE PUBLISHING COMPANY®
Denver • London • Sydney

Published by Love Publishing Company
Denver, Colorado 80222

Library of Congress Catalog Card Number 97-70238

CONTENTS

ACKNOWLEDGMENTS

*T*o Lonnie for your endless encouragement and reinforcement; to Martha Holden for your lifelong support that has made what I have done possible; to Beth Sulzer-Azaroff, my best teacher who taught me the true importance of positive teaching; and to the Jacksonville Police Department for your cooperative spirit with schools that sets an example for all police departments to follow.

—BHJ

*T*o Vickie for the support and encouragement you gave that made this project possible and for the evenings you spent alone while we put pen to paper; and to the Jacksonville Police Department for providing me with many years of employment and experience that I can now share to make schools safer.

—JPK

INTRODUCTION

*W*ith the increase in violence in U.S. society—and in schools—in recent years, educators have had to assume more responsibilities than just the teaching of reading, writing, and arithmetic. If children are to learn the basics, they must be safe and feel safe in the school environment. Educators must manage safe schools. This book provides techniques for doing so.

As Albert Shanker (1995) stated, "You can deliver a terrific curriculum, but if youngsters are throwing things, cursing and yelling and punching each other, the curriculum doesn't mean a thing in that classroom" (p. 8). In another article, Shanker reports that the majority of schools in the United States are plagued with violence (Raspberry, 1995).

With this "epidemic of violence" in society, as Lantieri (1995) aptly called it, it has become difficult for educators to assure that schools are safe havens. Schools mirror society's problems.

Zinmeister (1990) stated that if dangerous disorder is allowed to exist in our schools, children get a powerfully negative impression of society's interest in protecting them. Schools have to be sanctuaries, in which, at a minimum, physical safety is guaranteed.

In a ten-year follow-up to a 1984 report by Gary Bauer (the Under-Secretary of Education at that time) entitled *Disorder in our Public Schools*, Robert Maginnis provides some startling statistics. Nearly 135,000 guns are brought to schools each day, approximately three million crimes occur on or near school property every year, and one fifth of schools nationwide report student on teacher assaults (Maginnis, 1995). Hyman, Weiler, Shanock, and Britton (1995) reported that 71 gunshot deaths occurred in U.S. schools in 1990, and that number has likely increased in recent years.

Violence is widespread. A 1995 Louis Harris Associates poll of 2,500 public school students in grades 3 through 12 and 1,000 parents of public school students in those grades revealed that almost one fourth of the students had been involved in a physical fight at school (Maloney, 1995).

School violence, once largely confined to large cities, is now on the increase in communities of all sizes. In a 1994 National League of Cities Survey of 700 U.S. cities and towns, the largest cities reported a 55% increase in school violence over the past five years, medium-sized cities reported a 46% increase, and smaller cities reported a 31% increase (Maloney, 1995).

Threats of violence are not confined to junior and senior high schools. Sauerwein (1995) reported that educators and mental health specialists are seeing an increase in aggressive behavior even among children 10 years of age and under. One five-year-old kindergarten student, for example, took a loaded .22 caliber pistol to school. We, too, have seen an increase in aggressive behavior among young students. In our work, as a school official and a police official working with students with severe behavioral problems, the number of young students referred to us has risen dramatically in recent years. One seven-year-old referred to us for assistance had become so violent in an elementary-school building that the police were called, and it took four police officers to subdue the youngster, who had already been recruited for gang activity. A kindergarten student in a community in central Illinois was referred to us after bringing a gun to school for show-and-tell.

According to Kathleen Lyons, a spokesperson for the National Education Association, in an Associated Press article, August 25, 1995, "The number one concern of teachers right now is the need to have a safe school" (Associated Press, p. 19). Nevertheless, many school officials remain oblivious to some of the aggressive incidents that are occurring in their schools, and others choose to ignore such incidents. Both situations often lead to an increase in violence. Schools that tolerate low-level aggressive incidents usually see increases in high-level aggression. Typically, when schools ignore the problems of violence, the problems escalate, easily becoming out of control. Even those school officials who are aware of aggressive incidents in their schools and choose to deal with them often do not know how to deal with the problems appropriately.

It is our strong belief that coordination with local police is a must in dealing with the problems of violence in today's schools. Much attention has been focused in the legislative arena on students who bring guns to school and students who are disruptive. Much of the discussion has centered on the expulsion of these students. Although expulsion may be an immediate solution, it certainly is not a long-term resolution to the problem. Students who have been expelled from school typically cause trouble in the community and make more work for police departments.

Compounding the problem, they are not being educated to become productive tax-paying citizens. The solution rests not in expulsion but in keeping those students in safe schools. This book will provide educators with the tools to appropriately deal with aggression in the schools and to manage schools that are safe for all students.

It should be a common goal of school officials and law enforcement officers to keep students in a safe school environment and off the streets. To do so, schools and law enforcement cannot work in isolation but must be in concert with each other. The once prevalent attitude of school officials that the "schools are run by the schools" is now archaic and should, we believe, be discarded immediately. Just as we joined together in writing this book, it is our hope that everyone reading it will form such productive police-school partnerships.

References

Associated Press. (1995, August 25). Poll: Lack of discipline chief problem at schools. *Jacksonville (Illinois) Journal-Courier,* p. 19.

Bauer, G. (1984). *Disorder in our public schools.* Washington, DC: United States Department of Education.

Hyman, I., Weiler, E., Shanock, A., & Britton, G. (1995, March 1). Schools as a safe haven: Politics of punitiveness and its effect on educators. *Education Week, 14*(23), 48.

Lantieri, L. (1995). Waging peace in our schools. *Kappan, 76*(5), 386–392.

Maginnis, R. (1995). *Violence in the schoolhouse: A 10-year update.* Washington, DC: Family Research Center.

Maloney, M. (1995). How dangerous are our schools? *School Violence Alert, 1*(1), 7.

Raspberry, W. (1995, September 4). AFT's Shanker: Loss of discipline hurting education. *The (Springfield, Illinois) State Journal-Register,* p. 6.

Sauerwein, K. (1995). Violence and young children. *Executive Educator, 17*(3), 23–26.

Shanker, A. (1995). Classrooms held hostage. *American Educator, 19*(1), 8–13.

Zinmeister, K. (1990). Tightening crime for children's sake. *Education Digest, 55*(7) 32–35.

CHECKLIST FOR ASSURING A SAFE SCHOOL

*W*e begin this chapter with a checklist that educators can use to determine whether their schools are, indeed, doing everything they can to assure a safe environment for students and staff. An explanation of the checklist follows.

Is Your School Safe?

Policies

☐ Does your school have clearly written policies for the following?
- School crises
- Searches
- Guns and other weapons
- Hostage situations
- Safe physical intervention
- Time-out
- Dress code

☐ Did staff, parents, and, when appropriate, students have input into the development of these policies?

☐ Did your school work with the local police department in developing some of these policies?

☐ Were the policies thoroughly explained to all stakeholders?

☐ Does your school have a working agreement with the local police department and other appropriate agencies concerning these policies?

F acilities

☐ Does your school require all visitors to enter at one designated point?

☐ Is there someone who is responsible for monitoring that entrance and checking visitors in?

☐ Does your school have an alarm system or a procedure in place for when problems occur?

☐ Is there clear visibility of all school areas—the parking lot, inside the school, the playground?

☐ Have blind spots on the school premises been identified?

☐ Does your school provide adequate supervision of problem areas and blind spots?

☐ Is the school building well lit at night?

☐ Is the school area free of rocks and gravel?

☐ Are all windows and doors properly secured and checked at the end of each day?

☐ Is after-hours use of playground facilities consistently and closely monitored?

☐ Are periodic inventories made of school property?

☐ Are valuable items properly marked, locked, or secured?

☐ Are school files locked?

☐ Is someone designated to oversee school security procedures?

☐ Do law enforcement personnel monitor the school facilities before, during, and after school hours?

☐ Is a check of the building done by school personnel at the beginning and end of each day?

*S*tudents

☐ Have high and clear expectations been set for and conveyed to students, and are those expectations periodically reviewed?

☐ Are immediate and logical consequences rendered for rules that are followed or broken?

☐ Are students given adequate opportunities to be heard?

☐ Does the school provide students with opportunities for resolving conflicts peacefully?

☐ Are students given opportunities to gain recognition?

☐ Are students given opportunities to earn privileges?

☐ Are students taught appropriate behavior and coping skills?

*S*taff

☐ Are teachers provided with ongoing training and current information with regard to safety issues?

☐ Is a strong support system provided?

☐ Are teachers given opportunities to be creative and involved in professional growth activities?

☐ Are teachers given opportunities to share in decision making and to work together in school planning and goal setting?

☐ Does your school have a team of individuals trained to deal with crises?

As is apparent from this checklist, measures must be taken with regard to school policies, facilities, students, and staff to assure a safe and effective learning environment. All items in the checklist are important; all contribute to an environment that fosters learning. Additional safety and security surveys, checklists, and questionnaires also are available from Ronald Stephens (1995) in *Safe Schools: A Handbook for Violence Prevention*. Our rationale for including each item in our checklist follows.

Policies

School officials may think that violent or illegal acts will never happen in their school or may refuse to recognize that such activities already are occurring there. Some educators believe that if they ignore the problem of violence in their school, it will go away. Others do not want to admit to the community that their school has a problem with violence, fearing that if word got out about such problems in their school, the community members would think the educators were not doing their jobs. As a result of these attitudes, many school officials fail to develop policies for dealing with various types of crises.

Although educators may not want to admit it, violent acts can occur in any school, and policies must be in place for dealing with them. A personal anecdote highlights the importance of instituting crisis policies despite the arguments of those who say crises will not occur. We recall developing a hostage situation policy for a school and being laughed at by a fellow administrator for doing so. That administrator was adamant that there would never be a hostage situation in a school. Shortly after that policy was put into effect, however, a school in another part of the state experienced a hostage situation that resulted in a death.

All school personnel must realize that such situations *can* occur in any school.

According to Gaustad (1991, p. 13), "Denial on the part of administrators can paralyze a district while problems become deeply entrenched [and] far more difficult to deal with than if faced at an earlier stage." She further stated that all school officials tend to believe that they are invulnerable; that violent acts cannot happen to them.

Once educators admit that their schools have a violence problem or that their schools may have such a problem in the future, they must plan for possible crises. One of the most important ways to plan is through the development of written policies. According to Wanat (1996, p. 127), "School policies are the mechanism by which safe schools are created." With each discussion in this book we have included sample policies that schools can adapt or adopt for their purposes.

In addition to helping to assure school safety—their main purpose—such policies and procedures protect school districts in the event of a lawsuit. Courts always determine whether the district had a policy in place and whether the educators were following that policy. We recall an incident in which a student being bused to our school program sexually harassed a student who was attending the program from another school. The incident occurred on the bus. The parent of the student who was harassed was very angry with the home school district. Because our school had a policy in place for dealing with sexual harassment and consulted with the police, we were able to implement all of the steps in the policy and therefore kept the district out of court.

All school safety policies should be developed with input from staff, students (when appropriate), members of the school's parent advisory council, and members of relevant community agencies through a Coordinating Council.

Johns, Carr, and Hoots (1995) write about the implementation of a Coordinating Council. Schools should play an active role in bringing community resources together to discuss mutual concerns. The council should be composed of representatives of the police department, the local probation department, the state's attorney, the truant officer, local mental health agency, local family service agency, and any other relevant social agencies that are likely to work with the school. Schools should establish such a council and offer to host the meetings. The advantage of hosting the meetings is that other agencies are then visible within the school and can have important input into its operation. The Coordinating Council should meet on a regular basis to discuss issues of common concerns. In our area, the Coordinating Council assists in the development of policies and procedures and provides suggestions for school improvement. Such widespread input will help to ensure compliance and support of the policies.

One community agency that should always be consulted in the development of school safety policies and procedures is the police department. Detailed information about working with the police department is provided in Chapter 4.

Once school safety policies have been developed, they must be explained to everyone involved—parents, students, staff, and members of community agencies. If these individuals do not know the policies exist or do not understand them, the policies will not be useful. The policies and procedures can be explained at staff meetings, at student assemblies, at parent-teacher meetings, and during other opportunities available in the school system. Educators can create fun contests to test student knowledge about the policies.

Finally, it is important for schools to have a positive working relationship with the media in their area. Being able to explain the rationale behind certain policies in the media can assist in educating local community members and gaining their compliance and support.

*F*acilities

In our consulting work, we have been able to walk freely into almost any school building and through the halls without anyone stopping us. Unless we have chosen to check in at the school office, we have been able to wander around the school buildings unchecked. If we can do that, as we always tell school officials, anyone can—and not everyone is well meaning. In August 1995, for instance, in a small community in southern Illinois that had always been perceived as safe, "a gun-wielding father barged into a third grade classroom, waved the teacher aside and dragged his 8-year-old daughter off screaming and crying while other pupils hid under desks" (Associated Press, 1995, p. 9). Schools *must* create better ways to screen visitors.

To assure everyone's safety, all visitors to a school should be required to enter at one designated point (or two or three designated points in very large schools) that is monitored by someone responsible for checking visitors in. We recommend that all other school entrances be locked during the day so that people can enter only at the designated point(s). In our school, the receptionist's desk was moved to the hall inside the designated visitor entrance that remained unlocked during the day, so that visitors cannot come into the building without being seen by the receptionist. The receptionist was then trained on what to do if someone looked suspicious or became belligerent. In addition, a buzzer system was installed for use by the receptionist in emergencies.

We recommend buzzer systems for all schools. Such systems, which can be installed by an alarm company, simply consist of buttons hidden in strategic locations throughout the school building. In the event of a life-or-death emergency, one of the buttons can be discreetly pressed, sounding an alarm at the local police department. Generally, police can arrive at the building within a matter of seconds. In our school, the buzzer for the receptionist's desk, was placed under the middle desk drawer. Procedures for handling problem visitors are discussed further in Chapter 13.

Another important safety factor is good visibility of all school areas. All educators need to examine their building and grounds to determine if any blind spots exist. We recommend installing video cameras in hallways, other problem areas, and any blind spots. In one large high school we examined for blind spots, we observed that student lockers were set up in groups of four in a U-shape. Even if there had been hallway video monitors, a supervisor would not have been able to see a student hiding within the U-shaped area. In another school, students were known to hide in the unlocked janitor's closet. Potential problems could be avoided by the use of hallway monitors and by blocking access to off-limit areas.

In areas where problems have occurred, as well as in areas where they are most likely to occur, such as hallways, playgrounds with bushes, and parking areas, supervision needs to be increased. Sadly, many students today cannot be left unsupervised. Bullies and problem instigators tend to pick on students where adult witnesses cannot see their actions. Schools need to increase the number of hallway monitors, cafeteria monitors, and parking lot attendants they use so that all areas are adequately supervised. As an added precaution, all outside school areas should be kept free of gravel to prevent the possibility of anyone throwing a rock at a window.

To deter people from trying to break into schools after hours, all school buildings should be well lit at night, and expensive equipment such as videos, television sets, and projectors should be kept out of open sight. Further, all such equipment should be clearly marked as school property, for it is more tempting to steal unmarked equipment than that which is marked as the property of a school. Also concerning school equipment, all valuable items should be locked or otherwise secured when not in use. They should never be left in plain view for someone to take. In addition, schools should inventory all equipment and periodically check the inventories. Pieces of equipment that are not used regularly may disappear unnoticed if school officials do not periodically check their equipment inventories.

As mentioned previously, we recommend that all educators establish a positive working relationship with their local police department. It is important that the police patrol the school area during and after school hours. But in addition to the police checking the school, school officials should designate someone on the school staff to check the building at the beginning and the end of each school day. At the end of the day, that individual (typically a custodian) must be certain to check all windows and doors to see that they are properly locked. The twice-a-day check of the building will not only increase school safety but will also allow school officials to pinpoint when, for instance, gang graffiti appears or a piece of equipment has disappeared. Further, school policy must stress that anyone who enters the building after hours is responsible for locking anything they open.

*S*tudents

Extensive research conducted by Mayer and Sulzer-Azaroff (1991) has linked school vandalism to a lack of school rules or expectations. Decreases in vandalism occurred when school environments were made more reinforcing and less aversive. Mayer and Sulzer-Azaroff contend that some portion of aggression and destruction in the schools is tied to punitive environments.

Educators must set high and clear expectations for students. Research has shown that students respect educators who are firm, fair, and consistent. Students live up to the expectations of school personnel.

Not only must high expectations be set, but they must be clearly and repeatedly conveyed to the students. It is not enough to tell students the rules once and expect them to remember them. High school teachers and administrators are notorious for giving students a whole book of rules and then thinking that students actually read the book. Even if they do read the book, without reinforcement they are unlikely to remember the rules one week later. We advocate posting school rules so students can be reminded of them every day.

To reinforce rule-following, a system of rewards should be established. Students who follow the rules should be afforded special recognition and privileges. Likewise, a system of logical consequences for not following the rules must be established.

In addition, students should be given ample opportunities to be heard. Student Councils and Student Governments are appropriate forums. Along the same line, a means of peaceful conflict resolution should be in place for all students. To this end, many schools are establishing conflict resolution and peer mediation programs. Such programs offer students the opportunity to be heard, to listen to other students' viewpoints, and to solve their own problems nonviolently. Educators cannot assume that students know how to resolve their differences without violence. Students must be taught nonconfrontational methods for dealing with their anger.

Staff

It almost goes without saying that school personnel are an important factor in assuring school safety. To be effective, all educators must be provided with ongoing training and current information on all safety issues. Many schools have taken a no-tolerance approach to gang graffiti, drawings, and signs, but such an approach is ineffective if educators are unaware of what constitutes such a drawing or sign. Regularly scheduled training sessions by the police department can assist staff in becoming aware of the latest gang signs in their community. Such training would have prevented the situation in which a high school art teacher allowed a student to produce elaborate gang drawings in class simply because he did not know what they were.

The local police department can also assist school staff in learning to identify drug paraphernalia and drug lingo.

Teachers cannot be naive about drugs, gangs, or other inappropriate activities; when students know that teachers are knowledgeable, they are less likely to try to "pull a fast one."

According to Stover (1988), 3% of school staff are responsible for 50% of the behavioral referrals. Generally, those staff members have not been trained in effective behavior management. Teachers should be provided with the opportunity for effective behavior management training, and not just on a one-time basis. We have found that the most effective behavior management training is intense training followed by periodic follow-up sessions. The follow-up sessions provide an opportunity for teachers to receive feedback after testing the concepts they have learned and to receive ongoing support.

Support systems must be in place for teachers. How best to discipline a student is often a difficult and evolving decision, and teachers greatly benefit from having someone with whom they can discuss the problems they are having. Peer mentor programs and support groups provide valuable assistance.

Studies have shown that school morale is higher when the school discipline codes have been developed by teams of teachers and students (with input from administrators) than when those codes have been developed by administrators alone (Andrew, Parks, & Nelson, 1985). Teachers must have the opportunity to come together and identify schoolwide problems, brainstorm solutions to those problems, and establish procedures to stop the problems.

Indeed, it is essential that teachers be involved in all aspects of decision making in the school. We contend that if a school faculty is to operate in a true team spirit and feel that each individual has ownership in the school, all faculty members must be involved in the planning and goal setting for the school (Johns, Carr, & Hoots, 1995). Management from the top down does not promote a harmonious school.

We also advise that every school building have emergency response teams trained to deal with crisis situations. The team members should be trained in the use of safe physical(s) intervention and should be called on whenever a student's behavior is injurious or so out of control that personal and property safety are at risk.

The use of a crisis or emergency response team is explained in detail in Johns, Carr, and Hoots (1995). Briefly, such a team should consist of four to eight staff members who are well trained in safe verbal and physical intervention methods. These individuals must have a nonconfrontational manner when working with aggressive students. They must be proficient in the use of appropriate verbal interventions so that they can communicate with students in a way that will de-escalate situations whenever possible. Physical intervention is used only as a last resort, when verbal intervention has been unsuccessful. Appropriate self-defense strategies and physical intervention methods for a crisis response team are described in Johns and Carr (1995).

Having crisis intervention teams in place will send a clear message to students that violence will not be tolerated. It will also send a message to students, staff, and parents that the school has a strong commitment to the safety and welfare of students and staff.

References

Andrew, L., Parks, D., & Nelson, L. (1985). *Administrator's handbook for improving faculty morale.* Bloomington, IN: Phi Delta Kappa.

Associated Press. (1995, August 30). Gun-wielding man abducted daughter from school near Carbondale. *The (Springfield, Illinois) State Journal-Register,* p. 9.

Gaustad, J. (1991). Schools respond to gangs and violence. *Oregon School Study Council, 34*(9), 13.

Johns, B., & Carr, V. (1995). *Techniques for managing verbally and physically aggressive students.* Denver: Love Publishing.

Johns, B., Carr, V., & Hoots, C. (1995). *Reduction of school violence: Alternatives to suspension.* Horsham, PA: LRP Publications.

Mayer, G., & Sulzer-Azaroff, B. (1991). Interventions for vandalism. In G. Stoner, M. Shinn, & H. Walker (Eds.), *Interventions for achievement and behavior problems* (pp. 559–591). Silver Spring, MD: National Association of School Psychologists.

Stephens, R. (1995). *Safe schools: A handbook for violence prevention.* Bloomington, IN: National Education Service.

Stover, D. (1988). School violence is rising and your staff is the target. *Executive Educator, 10*(10), 15–16.

Wanat, C. (1996). Defining safe schools: A prerequisite for policy development. *Journal for a Just and Caring Education, 2*(2), 121–132.

RESOLVING CONFLICT PEACEFULLY

*I*f a school is to be a safe learning environment, students and staff must be taught to resolve conflict in a peaceful manner. Bullying, fist-fighting, and name-calling cannot be tolerated; students must be taught other ways to manage their feelings. Johnson and Johnson (1995) reported that preventing violence and resolving conflicts are interrelated. As they stated, violence prevention programs alone are not enough. Peaceful conflict resolution must be a part of the equation.

Violence often results from arguments among acquaintances or friends. Such incidents are commonplace in the news. Indeed, conflict is a necessary part of everyday life and can be productive if managed appropriately. Conflict often arises when individuals are committed to goals and relationships with other individuals. Depending on how it is managed, it can lead to either positive or negative outcomes.

According to Johnson and Johnson (1995), training students in conflict resolution not only helps schools become more orderly and peaceful but also improves instruction. Constructive conflict in the classroom can gain and hold student's attention, can increase their motivation to learn, can arouse their intellectual curiosity, and can improve the quality and creativity of problem solving.

Nearly everyone knows adults who still do not speak to someone they argued with years ago. Over the years, they have become more angry and have blown the original situation out of proportion. Sadly, they often die before they resolve their differences.

Attempts to resolve conflict with fists, loud voices, verbal put-downs, or weapons are not appropriate in school and are often counterproductive. Children must be taught that there are more appropriate alternatives for resolving conflict. Unfortunately, many parents do not model peaceful means of conflict resolution. It is up to educators to teach children methods of constructive conflict. Although, realistically, children may still have to resort to other methods to survive on the streets, educators must act under the hopeful assumption that the skills they teach will generalize to other situations. If students are taught that resolving conflict peacefully can result in more positive relationships with peers and in greater peace of mind, they will likely want to use the techniques increasingly in their everyday life.

Conflict, as mentioned, can be handled in positive or negative ways. Students must be taught positive ways. Conflict can have either creative or destructive results. Students must be taught ways of gaining the former. If handled appropriately, conflict can be a positive force for personal growth and social change. Johnson and Johnson (1996) believe, as we do, that schools will be safer learning environments if conflicts and their constructive management are encouraged.

We firmly believe that all schools should have a system in place for resolving student-student and staff-staff conflicts. Conflict resolution can also be used for student-staff conflicts if the staff member is willing to participate in the process. An adult mediator would be appropriate in this situation. However, we also believe that conflict resolution should not be the only response to an inappropriate act or anything as serious as a criminal offense. Logical consequences for inappropriate behavior should also be rendered. For example, if John beats up Bill, John has committed an illegal act and should, we believe, face the logical consequence of criminal charges. However, John and Bill must also engage in conflict resolution to resolve their differences so that such an incident does not recur.

The advantages of conflict resolution can be broken down as follows:

1. The process brings conflicting students or staff together in a neutral setting.
2. It resolves conflict through open communication.
3. It teaches cooperative decision making.
4. It ensures consistency and fairness.
5. It makes students responsible for their own actions.
6. It directly teaches negotiation skills and higher-level thinking. Life is full of situations in which individuals must negotiate; through conflict resolution, students learn that skill.
7. It brings closure to a problem, so that individuals do not hold grudges. Unresolved conflict leads to anger and hostility.
8. It opens lines of communication.
9. It ensures the respectful treatment of students. Students have the opportunity to be heard and to tell their side of the story.
10. Unlike suspensions and detentions, which remove students from a situation and allow them to escape

a problem, it shapes appropriate behavior by teaching students to face problems and resolve conflicts peacefully.

Conflict Resolution with an Adult as the Mediator

When instituting a formalized system of conflict resolution, school staff may want to start with a system in which an adult—a teacher, an administrator, or a social worker—conducts the mediation. The process should be used as a matter of course whenever two or more students are having a conflict with each other. The basic process we use, which we adapted from the work of Schrumpf, Crawford, and Usadel (1991), is as follows.

First, the parties in conflict are brought together. They are instructed to sit facing each other on either side of a table. The mediator sits at the head of the table. When two groups, such as gangs, are involved, two mediators may be needed.

The mediator opens the session by introducing himself or herself as the mediator and asking each disputant to introduce himself or herself. The mediator then provides the ground rules, saying that he or she will remain neutral and will not take sides, that the session will be confidential—nothing is to leave the room, that each party is to respect the other party by listening and by not interrupting when the other is speaking, and that both parties must cooperate in the process if the dispute is to be resolved. After stating the ground rules, the mediator obtains a commitment from each party to follow those rules.

The mediator then begins the process of gathering necessary information. He or she asks each disputant to tell his or her side of the story using words to the effect of,

"Will you each tell me what happened?" As the parties speak, the mediator listens, summarizes, and clarifies. He or she repeats statements made, rephrases to check accuracy, and sums up the disputants' statements. The mediator then asks if anyone has anything to add and repeats the process of listening, summarizing, and clarifying. When no one has anything further to add, the mediator restates both sides of the situation.

The mediator then brings out the parties' common interests by asking such questions as:

- What do you want?
- If you were in the other person's shoes, how would you feel?
- If you could ask the other person to do one thing, what would it be?
- What might happen if you do not reach an agreement?
- Why do you think the other person has not done what you want?

After gaining insight into the parties' common interests, the mediator summarizes those common bonds using phrases such as, "Both of you seem to agree that..." and, "It sounds like each of you wants..."

The mediator then asks the disputants to brainstorm solutions that might satisfy both parties. He or she should teach, or remind, the students of the rules of brainstorming: They should say any ideas that come to mind, they should not judge or discuss the ideas that are raised, and they should come up with as many ideas as possible. As ideas are raised, the mediator writes them down.

The mediator then asks the disputants to evaluate the options and come up with a workable solution. To reach this end, the mediator instructs the students to identify those points that have the best possibilities—that is, those that are reality based—and to work together to improve on those solutions. When an agreement is reached, the mediator asks the students to check again that it is appropriate, realistic, and mutually satisfying. The mediator then summarizes the agreement.

As a final step, the mediator obtains the commitment of each participant to follow the agreement. The mediator may do so by writing up the agreement and having the participants sign it or by securing an oral agreement. We have found both means to be effective. Once commitments are made, the mediator congratulates the parties for working to reach the agreement and asks the parties to shake hands. The mediator closes the session by providing the parties with a vote of confidence, saying something to the effect of, "I know that you will all abide by this agreement."

This process of conflict resolution with an adult as mediator typically benefits both the students and the adult mediators. Both learn to mediate. Often, as staff become comfortable with the mediation process, they begin to hold peer mediation sessions to deal with conflicts among staff members.

Conflict Resolution with Students as Peer Mediators

A significant number of peer mediation systems have been established in schools across the United States. The concept of children helping other children is an important perspective. Lane and McWhirter (1993) found that peer leaders had greater credibility than school staff in social interactions among students. Further, participants in peer mediation programs tend to feel more committed to the intervention's goals and tend to be more interested in producing change among their peers than are participants in staff-led mediations. Wade (1993), writing about a peer mediation program at an elementary school on the South Side of Chicago, encouraged schools to include a good cross-section of the student body—from at-risk students to straight-A students—when selecting students to train as peer mediators. However, the mediators chosen should be students with whom other students can relate. At-risk students who participate in the program can benefit by developing more prosocial attitudes toward conflicts.

Essentially, the same model is used as described for the staff-led mediations. Some schools use one peer mediator, some use two, and some use one mediator with an adult staff member as an observer. For the process to be used, however, students must understand and feel comfortable using the mediation process. We recommend that schools incorporate conflict resolution concepts into their curricula prior to setting up a mediation program.

The Teaching Students to Be Peacemakers Program, developed by Johnson and Johnson (1996), is one such program. In this research-based, 12-year spiral program, all students from Grade 1 to Grade 12 learn negotiation and mediation procedures. The six steps of this program as summarized in Johnson and Johnson (1996) are as follows:

1. Create, within the school, an awareness of students' interdependence and interaction.
2. Teach students to distinguish when conflicts are occurring and are not occurring.
3. Teach students a specific procedure for negotiating agreements.

4. Teach students how to use a specific mediation procedure.
5. Implement a peer mediation system.
6. On a weekly basis, continue training 1st through 12th grade students in procedures for negotiating and mediating. A few hours of training is not enough to teach effective conflict management.

Conflict Resolution for Staff

It is vital that all staff in every school set an example of being able to peacefully resolve conflicts. Not only do students notice when one teacher is not getting along with another teacher and often play that friction to their advantage, but, perhaps even more important, the climate of an entire school is in jeopardy when teachers are in conflict because teamwork is not in place.

Peer mediation systems can effectively alleviate such conflicts. Either staff members or the building administrator can serve as mediator. In our school, volunteer mediators were trained using Schrumpf's material (Schrumpf, Crawford, & Usadel, 1991). We recommend that all schools establish a system of peer mediation for resolving staff conflict. Sample guidelines for conducting peer mediation for staff are provided in Appendix A.

In summary, if violence is to be curbed in today's society, educators must not only model peaceful conflict resolution but teach their students the steps involved in conflict resolution. As Johnson and Johnson (1996, p. 10) stated, "Teaching students how to resolve conflicts constructively is one of the best investments schools can make."

✗*References*

Johnson, D., & Johnson, R. (1995). *Reducing school violence through conflict resolution.* Alexandria, VA: Association for Supervision and Curriculum Development.

Johnson, D., & Johnson, R. (1996). Peacemakers: Teaching students to resolve their own and schoolmates' conflicts. *Focus on Exceptional Children, 28*(6), 1–12.

Lane, P., & McWhirter, J. (1993). Conflict is inevitable, violence is not: Peer mediation in the schools. *Reform Report: A Monthly Publication of the Chicago Panel on Public School Policy and Finance, 3*(5), 1–6.

Schrumpf, F., Crawford, D., & Usadel, H. (1991). *Peer mediation: Conflict resolution in the schools.* Champaign, IL: Research Press.

Wade, A. (1993). Reporting reform: White Elementary finds mediator training works. *Reform Report: A Monthly Publication of the Chicago Panel on Public School Policy and Finance, 3*(5), 7–10.

COMBATING TRUANCY

*O*ne might ask why truancy is discussed in a book about safe schools. The answer is simple. Truancy is a symptom of larger school problems. Students may skip school because they do not believe that they belong to the school community; such students may look for other places or activities where they can belong, including gangs. Students may skip school because they want to test limits and see what they can get away with, a symptom that their school does not have clear expectations for students. As discussed earlier, a lack of clear expectations can result in an unsafe school. Further, students may not attend school because they feel unsafe there. They may be bullied, bothered with gang intimidation, or sexually harassed, or they may have had a sexual crime committed against them on the school grounds. According to Winters (1996), when students start skipping school, they are telling their parents, school officials, and the community that they are in trouble and need help. Educators who ignore truancy are, indeed, verifying that their school may be unsafe.

X *Community* Coordination

Truancy is not just a "school problem." It is a community problem. Many studies have indicated that high truancy rates equate to high crime rates. Kennelly (1994) reported that in Charleston, South Carolina, where the police pick up truant students and take them to school, daytime burglaries decreased by 43% between 1991, when the program started, and November 1994. Levine (1993) reported that 85% of all daytime crime is committed by school students and that prior truancy is the most common factor in the profiles of adult criminals. Truant students are more likely than children who attend school to be involved in criminal activity of all manner and description, including illegal drug activity, shoplifting, and other misdemeanors. They are also more likely to be involved in more serious crimes, such as drive-by shootings and other felonies. The truant child, in general, is more likely than children who attend school to be involved in problems in the community.

Goldstein and Huff (1993) reported that truancy is a characteristic of many criminal street gang members and that it is highly correlated with daytime burglary. Winters (1996) provided the following facts:

- During a recent period of time in Miami, more than 71% of the 13- to 16-year-olds prosecuted for criminal violations had been truant at the time of the crime.
- In Minneapolis, daytime crime dropped 68% after police started citing truant students.
- In San Diego, 44% of the violent juvenile crime occurred between 8:30 a.m. and 1:30 p.m.

Communities must band together with schools to combat truancy. In our school, a small core group that consisted of people from various community agencies met on a regular basis at the school to assist the school with problems it faced. As truancy became more and more a problem and a public issue, this coordinating council was expanded and became known as the Truancy Task Force. It included representatives from the school district, the local police, the office of the state's attorney, the city attorney's office, the Chamber of Commerce, the probation office, the county commissioner's office, the state's Department of Children and Family Services (DCFS), the local drug and alcohol treatment center, the Youth Attention Center, and other community businesses and industries.

The Truancy Task Force began to meet on a regular basis. At an early meeting, the following goals were delineated:

1. To establish a communication network among all community agencies that work with youth and clarify the responsibilities of each
2. To solicit ideas and support from the business community for how to convey to youth the importance of a good education
3. To establish an ordinance within the city that would allow the legal system to impose fines for blatant cases of truancy
4. To explore options and interventions for dealing with truancy that could be used within the city's schools to minimize suspensions and expulsions
5. To seek financial support for various intervention programs through grants and other sources

The task force met all of these goals. A communication network was established, with each agency having specific roles (see Appendix B) and the members of the task force serving as the unofficial liaisons between all of the represented agencies. A comprehensive list was compiled of each agency's responsibilities with regard to truancy. The list became an invaluable tool for the agencies for avoiding duplication of effort and services and for referrals. Major employers within the city began to provide input and ideas, as well as programs, to convey to youth the importance of education. A local restaurant, for example, began a program of hiring only those students who regularly attended school. A city ordinance was developed that made truancy a violation. The school district adopted new guidelines for combating truancy that aimed to minimize the number of suspensions and expulsions. And grants were received for various intervention programs.

As they worked to achieve these goals, the members of the task force became a team. They came to know one another on a first-name basis and developed into a strong network of like-minded people. This network continues today working both formally and informally to tackle difficult community problems.

The problem of truancy cannot be addressed by a single agency. Once community members realize that truancy is a problem that negatively impacts the entire community, a task force consisting of members of many community agencies can be formed and will likely be effective. Clear-cut goals are a must, as is determining the role of each agency as it pertains to youth services. In addition, concise truancy legislation (a truancy ordinance) must be sought if it is not already in place. (Truancy ordinances are described in detail in a later section of this chapter.)

In our community, the Truancy Task Force educated the city council about the problem of truancy in the city and then lobbied individual council members until they agreed to enact a truancy ordinance. Data from the first year that the community ordinance was in place showed an increase in average daily attendance at both the high school and the alternative special education school that served many students including approximately one third of the population that had a history of truancy. In the alternative school, the average daily attendance increased from 90.8% in 1993–1994 to 91.7% in 1994–1995. In the high school of 1,200 students, the average daily attendance increased from 91.3% to 92.2%.

Financial and community support are critical in the fight against truancy. In our community, educators helped gain this support by speaking about the truancy problem at meetings of local service clubs, such as Kiwanis and Rotary, and by soliciting local businesses and industries for funding for programs. They also discussed the truancy problem and the importance of keeping students in school with key community members.

Also important in combating truancy is developing and instituting alternatives to suspensions and expulsions. Educators send mixed signals when they work to keep children in school through, for example, task forces such as that described here and then suspend or expel them in large numbers. We encourage all schools to revise their policies so that suspensions and expulsions will be minimized. A number of alternatives to suspension are outlined in Appendix B.

One alternative we have found effective is rendering logical consequences for inappropriate behavior. A list of consequences is provided in Johns, Carr, and Hoots (1995).

*T*ruancy Ordinance

Children need to know that immediate consequences will be rendered in response to truancy and other inappropriate behaviors. Punishment rendered 6 months after a child commits an offense, when the incident is no longer fresh in the child's mind, will have little, if any, effect. Miller and Prinz (1991), who studied the relationship between stealing and truancy, found that schools and communities characterized by high levels of theft, disturbances, and vandalism also had a high level of truancy. Schools and communities that rendered immediate consequences for these behaviors saw a decrease in their occurrence.

At the state level in Illinois, and we suspect in most states, truancy is a difficult law to enforce. In this age of violent crime, the court system typically considers truancy to be a very minor offense. After the court is petitioned about a child, it generally takes many instances of truancy over a long period of time before adjudication is brought to a successful conclusion. By that time, the child has more than likely forgotten why he or she is in the court system and, in many cases, views the process as a joke.

In our experience, prosecuting attorneys have been reluctant to take truancy cases and the court has viewed them a waste of time! With the amount of resources needed to bring a truant student to full adjudication in state court and the overburdened docket of the court at this level, one can understand the reluctance.

Such problems are, however, greatly reduced when truancy is dealt with at the local level. Truancy is, in most cases, only a minor infraction of a municipal ordinance. One may ask, then, why bother having such ordinances? The answer is that charging a child for truancy under a local ordinance gives the school and law enforcement an immediate "handle" on a truant student. The consequences for a first offense, albeit minor, are immediate. The message is sent to the child that school is important and that he or she should be there. If ordinance violations continue to occur, the consequences can and should become more severe.

The typical consequence for a first truancy ordinance violation is a fine of $25 to $50, a certain number of hours of community service, or both. The fines and amount of community service are typically increased gradually if violations continue to occur. Remember that the purpose of a truancy ordinance, unlike parking ordinances, for example, is not to produce revenue but to send a message to parents and students that school is important and to deter students from being truant. Hence, the fines usually are rather low.

One might ask why community service should be ordered in the first place. In our city, community service was to be imposed in cases in which it was obvious that a student could not pay the fine. In practice, however, most of the city's truancy cases are being handled with community service as the punishment. In our opinion, students receive a more valuable lesson washing the windows at their school than by having their parents simply pay their fine. We have found community service work to be most effective when it is performed at the students' own school. Not only does it increase the students' "ownership" of the school (the students feel a sense of accomplishment when they see the results of the work they have done), but the students are also doing the work in the presence of their peers, which can have a strong deterrent effect on unapproved behavior.

In addition to focusing on truant students, all truancy ordinances should include a provision for parental responsibility whereby parents or caregivers who are active participants in the truancy of a child are also prosecuted. Be advised that such a provision can be controversial and should be worded carefully. (See the truancy ordinance included in Appendix B for wording that we recommend.) We are not advocating that parents be charged each time a child is truant. Many times, parents are not aware of or cannot control a truant. However, parents often are active participants, lying for their child so the child can miss school or simply allowing their child to miss school without a valid reason. We believe that consequences for the parent in such instances should parallel those for the child.

Most city and county probation departments are overburdened and probably will not welcome the idea of having to monitor the court-ordered community service of truant students. For this reason, we propose that the work be done at the students' own school and that school personnel—teachers, aides, maintenance staff, counselors, and so forth—who are already on the school property almost every day of the school year, supervise this work in place of the probation department.

We have experimented with such an arrangement in our city and have found it to work very well. A written agreement between the school district and the city was drafted in which the school district agreed to monitor and supervise all court-ordered community service for truant students. (An example of such an agreement is provided in Appendix B.) In accordance with this agreement, the school district assigned one person to monitor the community service program. This person insures that all students in the program show up when they are supposed to, assigns the work to be done by each student, and makes certain the work is completed satisfactorily. After a student completes the assigned community service, or when a student fails to do so, the school district reports back to the court. If a student does not perform the assigned community service, the court imposes an appropriate monetary fine.

In summary, we feel that local ordinances are a must for combating truancy. They provide immediate consequences to students who are truant. When coupled with a school-administered community service program, they are not a burden to the local probation and court system. They hold parents responsible when they are active participants in a child's truancy. And they announce to the community that being in school is important, which is, perhaps, their most valuable benefit.

Recognition of Good Attendance

In the effort to improve school attendance, penalizing students for not attending school is not enough; students must also be recognized for good attendance. If educators want to improve school attendance, they must reinforce that behavior. Many schools have, for years, awarded certificates for perfect school attendance for an entire year. However, such certificates are not enough incentive for some students to attend school, and for many at-risk students, more short-term recognition for attendance is necessary. Without it, a student may miss one day of school in September and feel no incentive to attend for the rest of the year because he or she has lost the possibility of perfect attendance. The following ideas for rewarding attendance have been successful in various schools across the country:

- Having monthly pizza parties for students who have had perfect attendance for the month. Certificates can be awarded at these parties. Some pizza parlors have donated the pizza when told the reason for the parties.
- Posting wall charts near the school's main entrance that show month-by-month those students who have had perfect attendance. Students like to see their accomplishments displayed in front of everyone who enters the building.
- Awarding coupons for fast food restaurants or discounts at video rental stores to students with perfect attendance monthly, quarterly, or on a semester basis. Restaurants and stores typically donate these coupons and discounts. Schools can work with their local Chambers of Commerce to set up these arrangements.
- Waiving the requirement of final exams for students who have had perfect attendance for a semester.
- Soliciting service organizations to provide financial awards to students with perfect attendance. In our area, for example, the Golden K Kiwanis Club awards $40 at the end of the year to each student in the alternative school who comes to school every day.
- Awarding students' attendance with points that are redeemable for books, T-Shirts, or other tangible goods available at the school store.

Recognizing students for good attendance sends students the message that their school wants them to be there and cares enough about them to recognize them for coming to school. In addition to improving attendance, such messages assist in assuring a safe school, for students have more respect for those they know care about them.

*P*arenting Classes

Parenting classes should be an integral component of any school's efforts to resolve the truancy problem. The schools and community must work with parents to motivate them to want to send their children to school. Winters (1996) encouraged schools to become more family-friendly by arranging convenient times and neutral settings for parent meetings, starting homework hotlines, training teachers to work with parents, hiring or appointing a parent liaison, and giving parents a voice in school decisions. These means of working with parents should, we feel, be a large part of the effort to motivate parents to ensure that their children attend school, but we would also add parenting classes to the list.

Parents are often blamed for the fact that their children are truant, but often the parents want their children to attend school but do not know how to get them to do that. The following scenarios are all too common: Johnny will not get out of bed and his mother does not know how to get him out of bed. Mrs. Jones drops her daughter off at the front door of the school but her daughter goes in the building and out the back door. In parenting classes we have taught, parents have told us some very sad stories: One single mother who was raising two sons did not know how to stop one of her sons from chasing her down the street and beating her; two parents with visual impairments did not know how to stop their daughter from climbing out of her bedroom window and running away.

According to a 1995 nationwide survey conducted by Honeywell, Inc. of 500 rural, suburban, and urban students and teachers on solutions for reducing violence among youth, both students and teachers believed that parenting classes and family support services were leading solutions to reducing youth violence (Maloney, 1995). We contend that such classes also help to decrease truancy.

Our community decided to tackle the truancy problem in a comprehensive manner rather than with a "quick fix" solution or a single solution. One component of the comprehensive plan was parenting classes specifically geared to parents who had truant children. The classes have been taught over a 6-week period each spring and fall with a different topic taught each week. The sequence of classes has been as follows: Building Your Child's Self-Esteem and Conflict Resolution, Living with a Teenager, Behavior Management, Dealing with Your Child's Truancy, Helping Your Child with Homework, and Panel on Agency Services that Can Help You.

All classes have been taught by volunteers who were members of the Truancy Task Force and active in many other activities in the city. As such, they were both aware of the truancy problem and knowledgeable about the resources of the community. Through teaching, the members of the task force have had an opportunity to show parents that they want to help, not penalize, them. For instance, by teaching the classes on behavior management, the assistant chief of police was able to show parents that he is a helper, not just an enforcer. Parents also benefit from the arrangement. One mother, who had been having items stolen from her house and feared for her family's safety, had been uncomfortable with the thought of reporting the information to the police. But after attending a class on gang prevention taught by a police officer, she reported the thefts and provided the police officer with useful information concerning gang activities.

Parents are encouraged to attend all classes, but the classes do not build on one another so it is possible to attend only some of them. Attendance records are kept.

How are parents identified for the classes? The area truant officer, of course, has the names of those parents whose children meet the criteria for truancy (in Illinois, the criterion is absence 10% of the time). However, the task force also targets parents of children who have been absent 5% of the time. School principals provide the names. Principals have reported that collecting such data is useful for them as well, for the information tells them of additional students with attendance problems. They are hopeful that identifying such students will serve as a preventive measure, encouraging them to improve their attendance.

The only funding for the classes has been $500 provided by a large manufacturer in Jacksonville. The money was used to purchase materials the parents can take home—specifically, small how-to booklets that accompany the subject matter covered in the classes. All other materials have been donated by the teachers of the classes. Another educational organization provided $50 to cover the cost of refreshments. For future sessions, the task force hopes to secure funding to provide a meal for the parents.

Door prizes, such as plants, meal certificates, and tablets of paper, have been given at the end of each session as a means of providing recognition to those parents who attend. Parents who attend all six sessions are awarded certificates.

Attendance records are provided to the truant officer so that the information can be reported to the judge for children awaiting court hearings.

As may be expected, it has often been difficult to get parents to attend. We have found the following measures useful incentives.

1. A great deal of publicity is necessary. We have been fortunate that our community newspaper and radio stations have been in full support of the task force's work and have publicized the classes well.

2. Letters are necessary and important in documenting that parents know about the classes and in encouraging participation. Our letters to parents are friendly yet let the parents know that attending the classes may help them in any future court hearing on their child's truancy. In addition, we have found personal contact to be very beneficial. For our classes, an initial phone contact is made and then all parents are called again on the morning of the workshops to remind them to attend. The truant officer also provides parents with frequent reminders about the classes.

3. Workshops should be held at a location the parents perceive as safe. We have held our workshops in a school located in a low-crime area of the city.

4. Transportation to the classes should be provided to parents who need it. For our classes, members of the task force provide the transportation. The parents benefit by having rides; the task force members benefit by getting to know some of the parents better as well as benefiting from the parents' attendance.

5. Food should be provided. Being served snacks or a meal will make parents feel more welcome.

We have found it useful to designate one or two people to coordinate the classes. These coordinators are members of the task force. Such individuals prepare and disseminate fliers about the classes; coordinate all written contact with the parents; coordinate the follow-up phone contacts with the parents; schedule the sessions and designate the speakers; prepare a news release for each session and disseminate it to all local news media; arrange the site for use; purchase all necessary materials; purchase refreshments for each session; check with speakers to determine what equipment will be needed and provide that equipment; arrange for door prizes; open, lock, and clean up the site; arrange transportation for parents who need it; record attendance; and prepare evaluations of the sessions.

Police Involvement

In some states, laws require schools to contact both parents and police when students leave the school premises without permission after the beginning of the school day. We feel that parents and the police should always be contacted in such a situation—even when legislation requiring their notification does not exist. We recommend the following steps:

1. Establish a school policy stating that parents and the police will be notified in the event that a student runs away from school. Place a statement to this effect in the school handbook.

2. Establish a notification procedure with the local police department.
3. Immediately notify the police and the student's parents whenever a student leaves the school grounds without permission.
4. Be prepared to give the police a description of the student including what the student was wearing; his or her hair color, length, and style; his or her height, weight, birth date, and address.
5. Encourage the police to return the student to school if he or she is found. When a student is returned to school, notify the student's parents immediately.
6. Establish a school policy stating that students who leave school without permission will, upon their return (whether on their own, by the police, or by parents), remain at school late (whether that day or the next school day) to make up the school time and academics that they missed while they were away from school.
7. Document the situation including the student's behavior and the staff notification of police and parents.

Combating truancy is a community problem; it must be addressed utilizing the resources of the school, police, courts, probation department, and the community at large. As one can see from this chapter, no single solution exists to solve the problem of truancy. A multifaceted, coordinated effort is critical.

References

Goldstein, A., & Huff, C. R. (1993). *The gang intervention handbook.* Champaign, IL: Research Press.

Johns, B., Carr, V., & Hoots, C. (1995). *Reduction of school violence: Alternatives to suspension.* Horsham, PA: LRP Publications.

Kennelly, J. (1994, November 18-20). The new crime stopper: You. *USA Weekend,* p. 24.

Levine, B. (1993, August 16). Tracking truants. *Los Angeles Times,* p. 16.

Maloney, M. (1995). How dangerous are our schools? *School Violence Alert, 1*(1), 1, 6–7.

Miller, G., & Prinz, R. (1991). Designing interventions for stealing. In G. Stoner, M. Shinn, & H. Walker (Eds.), *Interventions for achievement and behavior problems* (pp. 593–616). Silver Spring, MD: National Association of School Psychologists.

Winters, K. (1996). *Manual to combat truancy.* Washington, DC: U.S. Department of Education, Safe and Drug Free Schools Office.

WORKING WITH POLICE

A key element in maintaining and managing a safe school is having a healthy working relationship with the police agencies in the area in which the school is located. The local police agency is a reservoir of resources for a school and can provide assistance in many areas.

The relationship between the school and the police agency or agencies can range from formal to informal but will likely have elements of both a formal and an informal nature. As an example of a formal element, police representatives can sit on the local school coordinating council. An informal element would be the use of a liaison between the school and the police department, a police officer that the school can contact for answers to questions, program requests, advice on policies and procedures, and many other items that come up in the day-to-day operations of a school. The school–liaison officer relationship is discussed in more detail later in this chapter.

Services Provided by Local Police Agencies

The local police department can do much more for a school than respond to reports of thefts or broken windows. It can and will provide a wide range of assistance. The following are just a few examples of services most police agencies will provide to a school. Schools should not hesitate to contact their liaison officer if they are in need of these or other services.

Staff Training

Most police agencies will provide an officer to train school staff in a number of areas. Search and seizure, building security, personal security, and contraband are just a few examples.

Security Consultation

Most police agencies will provide an officer to determine the security needs of a school. Often suggested are alarm systems, mirrors, intercom systems, coded signals for help, and the efficient reporting of emergencies.

Liaison Officer

As mentioned at the beginning of this chapter, the liaison officer is someone in the local police agency that school personnel can contact whenever the school is in need of police assistance. To set up this relationship, school personnel should contact the local police agency to find out who in the agency would be willing to assist the school in this manner. Typically, a public relations officer, a D.A.R.E. (Drug Abuse Resistance Education) officer, or possibly a crime prevention or juvenile officer will be named. This officer should be contacted and a meeting arranged in which the needs of the school will be discussed. Once the relationship is established, the school should turn to this officer whenever the services of the local police agency are needed. Directing all requests to one person will typically result in better service than attempting to contact a different person each time there is a need for police assistance. Plus, working with a single contact person will make dealing with the many and varied services provided by law enforcement a much simpler task.

Provision of Other Resources

Most police agencies will provide schools with books, fliers, pamphlets, coloring books, and so forth, on a wide range of subjects including drug abuse, bicycle safety, personal safety, and building security. Generally, police agencies have direct access to state film and video libraries on a vast number of subjects. The liaison officer can locate and supply items from these libraries as they are needed. In addition, police agencies having D.A.R.E. and public relations or community policing officers are more than willing to have these officers provide instruction to students and staff on a wide range of subjects. State police agencies can also be tapped for information and resources. The larger the agency, the more resources it will have available.

Educators will find that most police agencies will be willing partners with schools once the schools demonstrate their interest in and need of police services and their sincere willingness to work with the police. After all, in the school setting, the goal of both agencies—school and police—is the same: to provide a safe environment for all students and staff. If a school does all it can to provide the safest environment possible, the police role will be lessened, and the police can concentrate their efforts elsewhere.

✗ *Guidelines for Filing Charges*

We believe that criminal activity should not be tolerated in schools and that students who commit crimes in schools should face the logical consequence of having charges pressed against them. However, we feel that schools must follow specific guidelines when pressing charges against students, as delineated below.

Guidelines for Schools in Working with the Police When Pressing Charges

1. One staff member should be designated as the contact person with the police, prosecuting attorney's office, and probation office.
2. The school should press charges only for true criminal situations—that is, for violations of the law—and only for crimes in which there is an adult witness. Any noncriminal behaviors should be handled by schools internally.
3. Before contacting the police about a crime, the staff member who is the police contact should talk with the adult witness (or witnesses) to verify the actual incident and the willingness of the witness(es) to testify about the perpetrator's behavior.
4. Next, the staff member should talk with the perpetrator, listening to his or her side of the story, and should provide the perpetrator with due process, or "fair treatment" according to the law.
5. After verifying the incident, the staff member should immediately call the police to press charges on behalf of the school against the perpetrator. We emphasize that the school, and not the victim,

should press the charges, thereby eliminating the possibility of intimidation, fear, and revenge. The staff member should provide data about the perpetrator to the police, including age, date of birth, and parents' address and phone number.

6. After notifying the police, the staff member should document the incident on a police incident report (see sample in Appendix C) and send copies of the documentation to the arresting officer, the state's attorney, and the probation office. An incident narrative should always be included on the form.

7. Finally, the staff member should inform the parents of all students involved (perpetrators and victims) of the incident or situation and the legal action taken by the school.

WORKING WITH THE JUDICIAL SYSTEM

*I*t is a sad truth that to maintain a safe school environment educators will, at times, have to turn to the judicial system for help. Violent, abusive, disruptive students who cannot be controlled within the confines of school rules and regulations will eventually have to be dealt with by law enforcement and the judicial system.

We earlier discussed the importance of schools' establishing and maintaining a close working relationship with local and state law enforcement agencies. Equally important is the need to form a close working relationship with members of various parts of the judicial system, namely, the court, the prosecuting attorney's office, and the probation department. In this chapter, we describe the role of each in dealing with students charged with committing a crime and the sequence of events that occur in the judicial system after a school presses charges.

*R*ole of the Court

It is important for educators to understand the role of the court, specifically of the presiding judge, in cases involving student crime even though they will seldom have reason, or opportunity, to speak directly to the court. In all court cases, the presiding judge has the ultimate say in any case that comes before his or her court. Judges differ greatly in the manner in which they handle cases that come before them. All judges, of course, must act within the purview of the law, but the personality of the judge and the situation and details of a case will dictate how that case will be handled. In most instances, the school will not have any direct input on how a case will be adjudicated. The judge relies on information provided by the prosecutor and the probation department in determining the best course of action.

All judges must remain fair and impartial. Attempts to influence their opinion before they make a determination of guilt or innocence are inappropriate and will not be allowed. For instance, educators may not call a judge to discuss a case awaiting adjudication. For a judge to engage in such a discussion would be unethical.

Role of the Prosecuting Attorney's Office

Educators will have the greatest impact upon the decision of the court when they work with and through the prosecuting attorney's office and the probation office. Further, their impact on these offices will be greatest if the documentation they provide is based on sound fact and written in a clear and concise manner with an absence of opinion and prejudice.

Consider this example: Mrs. Brown, a teacher at the Happy Days Middle School, observes two students in her class fist-fighting with both students pulling punches. Jason, one of the students, has a long history of getting into trouble, and Mrs. Brown would like to get him out of her class. Bill, the other student, has never before been in trouble in Mrs. Brown's class and is a good student. In documenting the school's incident, Mrs. Brown provides a long, detailed report about Jason, in which she relays his long history of problems. At the same time, she writes a glowing report about Bill stating that she is sure he did not mean to do what he did. Note: The report is the school's form, which is given to the police department.

This type of documentation would, for both students, be considered prejudicial. Mrs. Brown was attempting to influence the court's finding of guilt or innocence. Her report should have contained only factual information, not opinion. Documentation of all past incidents of disruptive and criminal behavior as well as examples of good behavior should be shared with the probation department, which would take that information into account when making its recommendation to the court concerning the proper disposition of the juvenile offender.

We strongly encourage the school staff member designated as contact with the police, prosecuting attorney's office, and probation office to contact the prosecutor with jurisdiction over the school's area to find out who in the office handles juvenile matters—the prosecutor or an assistant or assistants. The staff member should then discuss with that person the school's program for a safer school environment and should seek suggestions and advice on the best course of action to follow when the school finds itself in the position of needing court intervention for handling a situation with a student. We cannot stress enough the importance of learning what the prosecutor's office will and will not prosecute, for the school's perception of what is criminal may differ greatly from the prosecutor's perception. (See Chapter 6 for further discussion.)

Indeed, prosecutors may not press charges for some acts that are in violation of state or city laws. Consider the following scenario. Jason brings a one-hitter pipe (marijuana paraphernalia) to school. The school principal, Mr. King, immediately calls the police and presses charges against Jason because possession of a one-hitter pipe is unlawful in their state. However, when the case comes before the prosecutor, he immediately dismisses the charges. If Mr. King had previously established a working relationship with the prosecutor, he would have known that the prosecutor did not believe that particular offense was significant enough for prosecution and would have saved the time of the police department.

Whether or not the prosecutor's office will try cases such as the one just described, we believe that all schools should have in place clear policies that do not allow the possession of illegal items in the school. Such items should be confiscated and parents informed. In all such cases, the school should render consequences for the behavior.

Consider another example. Jim has been acting out of control in school and one day runs up and down the halls yelling, swearing, and hitting lockers. By the strict definition of his state's statutes, his behavior would constitute disorderly conduct. However, few prosecutors would accept that what Jim did was criminal behavior. Again, schools should have in place policies that will let students know what behaviors are unacceptable in school, as well as procedures for handling such acts when they occur.

In situations in which a student is charged with a criminal act and is awaiting adjudication by the court, the staff contact should meet with the prosecutor well in advance of the court date to discuss the incident and ensure that the prosecutor is fully informed of the facts from the school's perspective. All too often, with the busy schedules everyone has today, school representatives find themselves meeting with prosecutors 15 minutes before it is time to go to court. No one can communicate all the information about a case and the school's desires for outcome under those conditions! An early, less rushed meeting with the prosecutor will make the day in court a much easier experience for all school representatives involved.

*R*ole *of the Probation Office*

In most U.S. states and counties, the probation office both conducts presentencing investigations and monitors juveniles on probation. The judge reviews the presentencing investigation report when making his or her decision about how best to adjudicate the juvenile. In many instances, this report carries more weight than anything else in determining what will be done with the juvenile being tried. The presentencing investigation includes a thorough investigation of the subject's prior arrest and conviction record. It may include the investigators' opinions as to how the subject may respond to probation versus incarceration.

As mentioned earlier, the staff contact will have the most influence on the outcome of a case by discussing it with the probation office. To establish a close working relationship and open communication with the local juvenile probation office, the staff contact should call that office, determine which probation officer or officers have charge of juveniles from his or her school, and get to know this officer or officers. When a situation arises in which a student is being adjudicated, the contact person should talk to the probation officer about the facts of the case, the previous behavior of the student, and any insights he or she may have about corrective measures. A school can be much more open with the probation office than with the court. It is in this venue that the school's opinions, information about the student's behavior, and general knowledge of the student can and should be voiced. The information thus provided will assist the probation office in preparing its presentence recommendation for the court.

To reiterate, only firsthand knowledge of facts may be voiced in court. The school can, however, voice opinions and suggestions to the probation officer.

Taking the time to find out who in the judicial system will have control over cases a school may be involved in, before such situations occur, will save the school much time and trouble when the need arises to use the judicial system. Getting to know the local prosecutors and probation officers will be time well spent.

Sequence of Events from Commission of Illegal Act to Sentencing

We have prepared the following step-by-step sequence to help readers gain a better understanding of the events that occur from the time a criminal offense is committed by a juvenile until the case has made its way through the judicial system.

1. Student commits significant unlawful act.
2. School representative contacts the police.
3. School presses charges and arrest is made.
4. School representative contacts parents of student who has committed the criminal offense.

5. Police determine proper temporary disposition of offender (incarceration, in-home detention, release of student to parent or the school) based on the severity of the offense. A student incarcerated for a serious offense will have a detention hearing to determine whether the student should be incarcerated until the court date or released into the custody of a parent or guardian to await adjudication.

6. School provides documentation to police to support charges.

7. Police file a written report with the court (prosecutor).

8. School files written report with the police, prosecuting attorney's office, and probation office.

9. Prosecutor makes determination on whether charges will be dismissed or filed.

10. If charges are filed, an adjudicatory hearing, or trial, is held, in which a judge hears the case.

11. Upon a finding of guilt, a dispositional hearing is scheduled. Prior to the hearing, the school representative discusses the case with the probation officer, providing information that will assist the probation officer in making his or her presentence recommendation to the court. Sentencing is imposed at the dispositional hearing.

WHAT IS A CRIME?

*W*hy, one may ask, have we included a chapter in this book entitled "What Is a Crime?" Anyone can go to the statutes or ordinances of his or her state or city and look up the elements that must be present in a behavior for a perpetrator to be charged. In this chapter, we are not addressing the technical requirements; we are discussing the reality of what local law enforcement agencies and prosecutors typically accept as a crime to be adjudicated in their jurisdiction.

Educators must use good judgment and common sense in deciding when to involve law enforcement and the local prosecutor in filing charges for infractions of laws or ordinances by students. On occasion, it may seem easier to call the police when a student violates the law than to deal with the situation within school rules and regulations. But nothing will cause hard feelings between a school and the local law enforcement agency as quickly as wasting the officers' time! The local police know what crimes the local prosecutor will and will not prosecute, and schools should also have this knowledge. Running in the hallways may technically be disorderly conduct, and breaking a pencil may technically be criminal damage to property, but such infractions should not be cause to involve law enforcement. Although the temptation to call the police may be strong when a student with a long history of unruly conduct commits a minor law infraction, again, such minor infractions are best dealt with through sound school policies. The police and judicial system cannot solve all of a school's discipline problems.

It almost goes without saying that the local police are extremely busy people. In most cases, educators can rely on them for a quick, professional response to calls for assistance. But the police should be called only when they are truly needed. Educators must be careful to not "cry wolf."

Of course, to determine what behaviors warrant police intervention, one must know what constitutes a crime. To that end, we have compiled the following descriptions of common offenses. The descriptions were derived from the Illinois Revised Statutes but are typical of descriptions in statutes across the United States. We recommend that readers consult their own areas' statutes and ordinances to determine any differences from the Illinois Revised Statutes.

Descriptions of Common Offenses

Assault

A person commits an assault when, without lawful authority, he or she engages in conduct that places another person in reasonable apprehension of receiving a battery. The victim is in fear of being injured but actually receives no physical injury. Assault is a misdemeanor. With regard to assault by a person on school premises, if the person uses a deadly weapon or knows the person he or she is assaulting is a teacher, the crime becomes aggravated assault. Aggravated assault is a more serious misdemeanor.

*B*attery

A person commits battery if he or she intentionally or knowingly, without legal justification and by any means, causes bodily harm to an individual or makes physical contact of an insulting or provoking nature with an individual. Battery is a misdemeanor.

In crimes committed by a person on school premises, if the person uses a deadly weapon, is hooded or robed to conceal his or her identity, knows that the individual harmed is a teacher or other person employed in the school, knows that the individual harmed is pregnant, or knows that the individual harmed has a physical disability, battery becomes aggravated battery, which is a felony. Aggravated battery is more serious than battery. Additional statutes exist for heinous battery and aggravated battery with a firearm.

*T*heft

A person commits theft when he or she knowingly obtains or exerts unauthorized control over property owned by someone else, obtains control over the property of another by deception, or obtains such control by threat. Theft is a misdemeanor if the value of the property stolen is less than $300. It is a felony if the value is greater than $300.

*C*riminal Damage to Property

A person commits criminal damage to property when he or she knowingly damages the property of another without that person's consent. If the damage is less than $300, the crime is a misdemeanor; if it is more than $300, the crime is a felony.

Criminal damage to state-supported property, such as public school property, is a separate offense, for which additional statutes have been written.

Disorderly Conduct

A person commits the offense of disorderly conduct when he or she knowingly (1) acts in such an unreasonable manner as to alarm or disturb another and to provoke a breach of the peace, (2) transmits a false alarm to the fire department, (3) reports a false bomb threat, or (4) falsely reports a crime.

Criminal Behavior Requiring Police Notification

Any incident on school premises that involves a student striking another student or a teacher, that involves weapons, drugs, the possession of stolen property, or damage to school property of a real nature, or that involves theft should be reported to the local police agency without delay. Other criminal offenses may also be serious enough for police involvement, but those just cited are the most common.

When an offense that would typically warrant police intervention is committed by a student under the age of 12 or by a student with significant intellectual impairments, a prudent course of action is to consult with the local law enforcement agency about the situation. Policies and procedures for youthful offenders and for those with intellectual impairments vary greatly from state to state. Whether the police will intervene will generally depend on the seriousness of the crime or on the student's history of criminal activity.

Consider the following scenario. Ten-year-old Jeremy, in a fit of anger, is in the lunchroom and stabs Jason with a fork, causing significant bodily harm. The building administrator is not sure whether she should call the police because of Jeremy's age. We would recommend calling the police, explaining the situation, and letting the police make the determination on whether they will respond. Regardless of law enforcement's response, the administrator should document the incident in accordance with the school's safety policies and procedures. In our community, this incident would have been handled by the police, but the same response might not be the case in other communities.

Suggestions for forming a liaison with the local police agency were provided in Chapter 4. Schools should not hesitate to contact the local police authority when the need arises, but we urge all schools to use sound judgment in doing so. As mentioned previously, taking the time to learn what the local criminal justice system will and will not accept as prosecutable will ultimately save both schools and the police a lot of time and grief.

We recommend that every school district prepare a listing for administrators and teachers of what constitutes criminal behavior in their area. We have included in Appendix D the list prepared by our school district. The contents of the list will, of course, vary from state to state.

DRESS CODES

With gang activity present in so much of the United States today, we feel that establishing and enforcing dress codes is a necessary component of assuring a safe school. Too many students have been shot for innocently wearing the wrong color or the wrong jacket to school. However, we must emphasize that instituting a dress code alone will not solve the problem of violence in the schools; it is only one part of the solution.

Legal Issues

At the same time that we support dress codes, we acknowledge that schools must achieve a balance between the students' First Amendment right of free expression and the schools' responsibility to provide a safe and secure learning environment. Courts have consistently affirmed both the authority of school personnel to maintain a safe environment and students' civil rights. According to Lane and Stine (1993), the U.S. Supreme Court case *Tinker v. Des Moines* (1969) set the stage for current debates over dress codes when the Court declared unconstitutional the disciplining of students for their symbolic expression of opinion unless such expression could be shown to have caused a substantial disruption of the school's routine. In summary, schools must show that particular apparel could cause a substantial disruption of the school's routine.

In *Baxter v. Vigo County School Corporation* (1994), a Seventh Circuit court banned an elementary-school student from wearing T-shirts that read "Unfair Grades" and "Racism." The student's parents protested, stating that the school principal, in forbidding the student to wear the shirts, had violated her right to free speech. The court stated that previous cases involving students' rights to free speech indicated that age is a relevant factor in determining that right of the student. Because it could not conclude that this young child had a clearly established right to free speech, the court dismissed the matter. Thus, the age of the student continues to be a relevant factor that schools should consider.

Lane, Richardson, Van Berkum, and Swartz (1995) cautioned school districts to show, in dress codes, a connection between disallowed appearance and negative behavior or distraction from the educational function of the school. They stressed that schools should not judge students only on appearance. In their opinion, dress should be included as unacceptable in a school dress code only if it can be directly related to an inappropriate behavior that disrupts the school environment.

In 1994, the California State Legislature enacted a statute authorizing schools to adopt uniforms. The legislators who supported the statute believed that apparel related to gangs was hazardous to the health of students and the safety of the school environment. The statute, they contended, would protect students from being associated with any particular gang (Day, 1994). Other states have since adopted or are studying the possibility of adopting similar legislation.

Schools, we feel, do have the right to assure that nothing in the environment is disruptive to the educational process. Dress codes citing unacceptable clothing are thus an important component to managing safe schools.

Once a dress code is developed, it is important for the school district to have an attorney review all of the policies and procedures related to the dress code to ensure that they are fair and consistent with local laws (Stephens, 1993). In addition:

1. Students and their families should be made fully aware of the dress code and the reason for it.
2. Dress codes should be applied uniformly to all students.
3. Dress codes should address those items of clothing that are not typically worn by the student population as a whole.
4. Dress codes should be as specific and precise as possible.
5. Dress codes should not include references to specific sports teams because of the common practice of wearing apparel advertising sports teams. Many students wear such apparel; it is very prevalent in stores across the nation. However, if a student comes to school in a jacket depicting a sports team and is talking about the fact that he or she is wearing the jacket to advertise he or she is gang-affiliated, the student should be told that such talk is not appropriate and should be given a consequence.
6. Some type of appeal procedure should be in place and described in the dress code.

The following is a sample dress code that we feel addresses the majority of issues of concern in student dress today. Note the inclusion of a "Purpose" section to inform students, and their families, of the reason the code was instituted.

Sample School Dress Code

Purpose: Our school believes that it is important to define the type of attire that will promote a positive self-image among our students and will present a positive impression of our school to our community.

Apparel Advertising Substance Abuse

- No liquor, tobacco, or drug words will be permitted on any item of clothing.
- No pictures of such will be allowed.

Apparel Depicting Rock Groups

- Names of groups and/or concert dates are acceptable.
- Attire depicting skulls, violence, obscene words or gestures, satanic symbols, profanity, or sexual innuendos are not acceptable.

Gang Symbols and Tattoos

- Any staff member who suspects that a symbol on a student's apparel represents a gang will immediately refer the apparel for ruling by the Dress Code Committee (discussed later in this document).
- Tattoos must conform to dress code guidelines. If a tattoo does not do so, it must be covered by clothing, with a Band-Aid, or with some other covering.

- If a student wears clothing or accessories determined to be gang attire, he or she will be asked to wear the item inside out or to remove it for the day. (A school-supplied clothing item will be provided, when appropriate, for the student to wear in place of the prohibited item for the rest of the day.) If a student is asked to remove an item of clothing, that item will be given to the student to take home. Should the item be worn a second time, the item will be confiscated. In such instances, a contraband receipt will be given to the student and the student's parent will have to come to school to pick up the item.
- Commercial clothing, such as Starter clothing and sports team logo clothing, is acceptable. However, if a student makes a comment that an item of commercial clothing is a gang symbol, then the item will be considered gang related and the procedures for gang concerns, above, will be followed.

General Apparel

- Miniskirts, halters, short shorts, spandex, tank tops, half-shirts, midriffs, see-through tops, and fishnet and tube tops are not acceptable.
- Ripped jeans are acceptable as long as no part of the torso or thigh is showing.
- Shorts and skirts must be mid thigh or lower when a student is seated.
- Spandex is acceptable when worn under acceptable clothing.
- Cowboy boots are not acceptable.
- Boxer shorts are not acceptable when worn as shorts.
- Clothing revealing any personal and/or private body parts is not acceptable.

Accessories

- Coats, caps, and sunglasses are not allowed in the classroom or at assemblies.
- Book bags are to be placed in the hall during the school day. To assure the safety of all students and staff, book bags will be searched at intermittent times throughout the school year in accordance with the search procedures of the school.

Procedures to Be Followed When Inappropriate Attire Is Worn

If a student wears inappropriate clothing as defined in this dress code, the item must be worn inside out for the rest of the day or removed. In the latter situation, the student will be given a school-supplied clothing item to be worn for the remainder of the day.

Dress Code Committee

- This committee has several purposes. First, students who have questions about the acceptability of an item of clothing may present it to the committee before wearing it to obtain the committee's ruling. Second, students may use the committee as a forum for appealing dress code decisions that they believe are unfair. Before approaching the committee to appeal a decision, a student must discuss his or her concern with a teacher. If the teacher believes the concern is legitimate, the teacher and the student may then bring the issue to the committee. Third, staff members who have questions regarding the acceptability of a specific clothing item a student is wearing may bring their questions to the committee. All decisions of the committee are final.

- The Dress Code Appeals Committee will consist of a school administrator and seven other members of the school staff.
- Hearings of the Dress Code Appeals Committee will be held at 1:50 p.m. twice a week as needed.
- Two members of the committee will be assigned the responsibility of assuring that the committee meets when needed and that a schedule of the meeting times is posted in a visible place.
- The committee will keep a record of the items brought before it and the rulings determined. With that information, the school dress code will be updated each year and a copy provided to each student, each student's family, and all school staff.

References

Baxter v. Vigo County School Corporation, 26 F.3d 728 (7th Cir. 1994).

Day, R. (1994). *Legal issues surrounding safe schools.* Topeka, KS: National Organization on Legal Problems of Education.

Lane, K., Richardson, M., Van Berkum, D., & Swartz, S. (1995). Gang attire, student rights, and school safety. *Illinois School Law Quarterly, 15*(3), 115–123.

Lane, K., & Stine, D. (1993). Student dress codes. In W. Camp, J. Underwood, M. Connelly, & K. Lane (Eds.), *The principal's legal handbook* (pp. 23–28). Topeka, KS: National Organization on Legal Problems of Education.

Stephens, R. (1993). School-based interventions: Safety and security. In A. Goldstein & C. R. Huff (Eds.), *The gang intervention handbook* (pp. 219–256). Champaign, IL: Research Press.

Tinker v. Des Moines Indep. Community School Dist., 393 U.S. 503 (1969).

SEARCHES
IN SCHOOLS

Goal #7 of the Goals 2000: Educate America Act (Public Law 103-227, 1994) states: "By the year 2000, every school in the United States will be free of drugs, violence, and the unauthorized presence of firearms and alcohol, and will offer a disciplined environment conducive to learning." If schools are to meet this goal of freeing the learning environment of contraband, especially dangerous contraband, they will need to have procedures in place that will assist educators in creating such a safe environment. To that end, many schools are implementing search procedures.

We believe that appropriate searches conducted with legally correct methods are an important component of assuring school safety. Indeed, searches can be a powerful tool for keeping safety in a school. However, we feel that searches are appropriate only in cases in which there is reason to believe a rule violation has occurred that is compromising the safety of the students and staff. We also believe that all schools should have in place procedures for all types of searches. Those should be clearly delineated in the school handbook. A sample procedural statement for school searches is included in Appendix E.

Legal Issues

The Fourth Amendment prohibits unreasonable search and seizure. Thus, all educators, before conducting any school searches, must understand what constitutes a reasonable search. The U.S. Supreme Court detailed the requirements for school officials in conducting a legally appropriate search in 1985 in the landmark case *New Jersey v. T.L.O.* 469 U.S. 325, 340, 105 S. Ct. 733 (1985). A New Jersey court had found a school principal's search of a student's purse, after a teacher saw the girl smoking in the girls' restroom, to be reasonable and appropriate. The Supreme Court, when it eventually heard the case, supported the ruling and, in its decision, established the following important school search precedents.

First, the Fourth Amendment, the Court ruled, does apply to school officials, and school officials, acting as representatives of the state, are responsible for providing a safe environment conducive to education (Day, 1994; Dise, Iyer, & Debler, 1994). Second, the Court set a two-pronged standard for school searches that was in keeping with the Fourth Amendment: The search must be justified at its inception and it must be reasonable in its scope (Day, 1994). A school search, the Court determined, is justified when there is "reasonable cause" to conduct the search to maintain discipline in the classroom and on the school grounds. It included the violation of school rules as a reasonable cause for a search (Day, 1994; Dise, Iyer, & Debler, 1994). The reasonability of the scope of a school search is discussed later in this chapter.

The Supreme Court has also ruled on another case involving school searches. In a 6-3 decision on June 26, 1995, the Court ruled that the Vernonia School District,

(U.S. Supreme Court No. 94-590, 1995) in Oregon, could institute a random urinalysis policy for student athletes. The policy required that both students who wished to play sports and their parents sign a form consenting to the student drug testing. The Court's majority opinion, written by Justice Antonin Scalia, was based on three factors: (1) the decreased expectation of privacy for students in school, (2) the relative unobtrusiveness of the search to be conducted, and (3) the severity of the need to be met by the search. The major consideration of the Court in reaching its decision was the context of public schools, which are to act as the "guardians and tutors" of the students entrusted to their care. Thus, the Court set additional standards for educators to follow when considering the appropriateness of school searches.

A Legally Correct Search

So what must school administrators and staff need to know to conduct a legally correct search? First, they must determine whether there is reasonable cause for a search. Several authors who reviewed *T.L.O.* and subsequent cases reached the following conclusion: To establish "reasonable cause," a school administrator must weigh the evidence presented in the suspicion of a rule violation. Dise, Iyer, & Debler (1994) noted that reasonableness has been upheld in court when corroborating information has linked an individual with a suspected violation.

The following are some examples of reasonable cause for a search: a student overhears another student arranging a sale of drugs at school and reports the incident to a teacher or administrator; a staff member witnesses a student suspiciously passing something that appears to be contraband to another student; a student with a prior history of established drug violations is seen in the restroom during class time without a pass and appears nervous upon being seen; staff detect the odor of marijuana surrounding a student; a student carrying a clear plastic bag and wad of bills becomes nervous and tries to hide the items when a staff member notices them; a school bag makes a metallic thud when a student places it on a shelf and a frisk of the outside of the bag reveals an object that appears to be a weapon (Sorenson, Cambron-McCabe, & Thomas, 1993; Day, 1994; Dise, Iyer, & Debler, 1994).

Several authors have noted that a student's past involvement in rule violation can be considered when evaluating the reasonableness of a search (Sorenson, Cambron-McCabe, & Thomas, 1993; Day, 1994; Dise, Iyer, & Debler, 1994). In addition, the credibility of corroborating information and the motivation of the information source should be considered (Dise, Iyer, & Debler, 1994).

The second consideration that administrators and teachers need to evaluate when considering searching a student is, as stated in *T.L.O.,* the reasonableness of the scope of the search. Included here is consideration of a number of factors: the age and sex of the student to be searched, the nature and severity of the violation, the area to be searched, the time and place of the search, who will conduct the search, the discipline history and record of past behavioral incidents, probative value and reliability of the information used as a justification for the search, and the method of search (Sorenson, Cambron-McCabe, & Thomas, 1993; Day, 1994; Dise, Iyer, & Debler, 1994).

The age of the student must be taken into account to determine whether the inappropriate activity is reasonably age related (Sorenson, Cambron-McCabe, & Thomas, 1993; Dise, Iyer, & Debler, 1994).

When determining the type of search (body search, use of a metal detector, search of a personal item such as a book bag, purse, locker, desk, automobile, or bus seat, and so forth), the nature and severity of the violation should be evaluated and matched with the appropriate search procedure. We do not recommend that school personnel conduct strip searches of students or searches that involve the removal of more than outer clothing. Should a situation arise in which the need for such a search is deemed appropriate (for example, when there is a strong suspicion that a student is concealing drugs or weapons in or on a body part that will not be checked in a school body search), we recommend that local law enforcement be called.

However, in *Cornfield v. Consolidated High Sch. Dist. No. 230* (991 F.2d 1316 (7th Cir. 1993)), a strip search conducted by school administrators was ruled appropriate. As described by Day (1994), a student was suspected of having drugs concealed in the crotch of his pants and the school administrators believed that a pat-down search would have been too intrusive and ineffective. Thus, two male administrators escorted the student to the boys' locker room and conducted a strip search. No other observers were present. As the student undressed, the administrators observed from a distance. They refrained from physically touching the student and did not subject him to a body cavity search. The administrators allowed the student to put on a gym uniform while they searched his other clothes.

The area to be searched should be limited to that encompassing the suspected violation. However, as Dise, Iyer, and Debler (1994) cautioned in cases of perceived danger, the school must search all areas that could be potential areas for hidden contraband.

With regard to the method of search, in any situations of potential immediate danger, such as threats of bodily harm with a weapon, the search method should be as inclusive as necessary to protect the students and staff. Sorenson, Cambron-McCabe, and Thomas (1993) stated that the methods must be balanced against the necessity or purpose of a search.

How to Conduct a Body Search

Many school personnel do not know how to conduct a body search in a legal and appropriate manner. For that reason, we provide the following step-by-step guidelines.

1. The staff member who suspects a problem must ascertain whether there is reasonable cause for requesting a search. Several examples of reasonable cause were given previously. Other examples include a student telling a staff member that another student has contraband; bus driver reporting that a match was lit on the bus or that he or she smelled smoke on the bus; a student boasting about having contraband.
2. If the staff member believes there is reasonable cause, he or she should ask the student to speak to designated school officials in a room or area that is appropriate for conducting a search. The search should not be visible to other students. However, at least one adult witness should be present. Without witnesses, there is little except a student's honesty to stop the student from later claiming that the of-

ficial conducting the search did something inappropriate.

3. The student should be escorted by a team of at least two staff members to the area at which the search will be conducted. The student should never be let out of sight or given any opportunity to pass something to another student, to go to a locker or bathroom, to remove items from his or her pockets, or to drop or throw items away before the search. Further, the student should not be allowed to pick up his or her coat or jacket, school bag, purse or other personal belongings; staff members should carry those items for the student if they are needed for the search.

   The group should make no stops on the way to the designated area. We strongly recommend that the staff members walk beside or behind the student. Walking in front of the student greatly increases the likelihood that the student will be able to pass something off or throw it in the garbage along the way.

4. Once the group is in the designated area, the staff should place the student's personal belongings in one area of the room some distance away from the student. The official in charge of the search should explain to the student that a search must be conducted because school officials have reasonable cause to believe the student has contraband on his or her person or in his or her personal belongings. Again, a team of staff members should always be involved to provide witness to the procedure and to offer emergency assistance should the student become aggressive.

5. The staff conducting the search should put on latex gloves, a safety measure that will help to protect them from infectious contact with such items as needles concealed in pockets.

6. The actual body search should then be conducted. The team leader should ask the student to remove any outer clothing, such as a coat, sweater, or jacket. Such clothing should be placed with the student's other belongings to be searched later. Next, the student should be instructed to pull out the inside linings of the front pockets of his or her pants, dress, or skirt and then to remove his or her hands from the pockets. To prevent students from trying to conceal small items from their pockets in their hands as they pull the pockets out, students should be instructed to keep their hands open and release the pocket liner for staff to inspect. The contents of the pockets should be placed on the floor or in an area designated by the team leader. All pocket contents should be kept in full view of all staff. Back pant and skirt pockets should be checked next, followed by shirt pockets. If the student has a wallet or purse, the team leader should ask the student to open all of its compartments. Staff witnesses should verify the contents by orally stating them in front of the student and others participating in the search to prevent the student from later saying that the staff took a personal item or planted an item.

All of the items found should be examined carefully. Students may hide items in necklaces or in corners of their pockets; drugs or weapons can easily be taped to the inside of sleeves; drugs can be concealed inside felt tip or ink pens or other items. Each item should be searched with deliberation.

Next, the team leader should pat down the sleeves of the student's shirt or dress and ask the student to pull the shirt or dress tight across his or her chest, stomach, and waist area to reveal any concealed items.

The student should then be asked to take off his or her shoes. Staff members should search the inside of the shoes.

Finally, the team leader should ask the student to pull up his or her pant legs. The team leader should pat the student's legs from just above the knee down and should then check the student's socks.

7. While the team leader is conducting the body search, the other members of the team should be sure to remain in the room. As mentioned earlier, they serve as witnesses and as a safety precaution.

8. After the body search is completed, team members should search the student's school bag, coat, jacket, sweater, and other personal items. The search should be conducted in front of the student so that the searchers and witnesses can verify the contents and prevent the student from later saying that staff members took or planted any items.

9. If contraband is found, it should be confiscated immediately and a contraband receipt given to the student.

10. If the contraband is considered illegal (such as bullets, a gun, or drugs), the police should be notified immediately. They will confiscate the items and initiate legal charges. Contraband items that

are not illegal to possess but are inappropriate for school, such as pocket knives and drug paraphernalia, should be held by the school. In our opinion, students should not be given the ability to retrieve such items. Again, a contraband receipt should be issued for any item that is kept.

11. Parents should be informed that a search has been conducted and should be told of the confiscation of any items.

12. All details of the search should be documented, including the reasonable cause, the team members involved, the contraband found (or not found), and the cooperation level of the student. The documentation should be placed in the student's file. A sample search and seizure report is included in Appendix E.

13. If contraband has been found, school officials should initiate discipline procedures.

*H*ow to Conduct a Locker Search

Because lockers may, at times, need to be searched, a statement such as the following should be included in all school handbooks: "Lockers and desks are defined as school property. They are available for temporary student use but will be subject to periodic unannounced checks for unauthorized items." The following are step-by-step guidelines for conducting a locker search.

1. Both the student and adult witness(es) should be present at the time of the search. The student and adult witness(es) should observe while another staff member opens the locker and conducts the search.

2. The school official conducting the search should start at the top shelf of the locker and work his or her way down. The school official should remove items from the locker one at a time.

3. The locker items should be searched carefully, in full view of the student and adult witness(es), as they are removed from the locker. Lighters, pens, eyeglass cases, hatbands, and cigarette packs should be checked carefully.

4. No items should be put back in the locker until all items have been searched.

5. The school official should not stop searching just because something is found. All locker items should be examined.

6. Any illegal items found should be reported to the police and the student's parents. The police will confiscate illegal items and initiate legal charges.

7. Any inappropriate items, those that are legal but inappropriate for school, should be confiscated and a contraband receipt issued. The parent will be informed of the incident and must retrieve the item from the school.

8. All aspects of the search should be documented in writing.

Confiscated Contraband

All schools should have in place a procedure for handling contraband confiscated from students that is legal but inappropriate for school. Although we touched upon the procedure we recommend in our discussions of different types of searches, we include here a more detailed listing. These procedures relate only to legal contraband; illegal contraband should be turned over to the police.

1. The school handbook should clearly state school expectations regarding what is and is not contraband, such as cigarettes, lighters, matches, chewing tobacco, or items designed to harm self or others.
2. Any item that is confiscated and deemed to be contraband should be tagged and kept in a secure place at the school. The student from whom the item was taken should receive a contraband receipt that states the nature of the item and where it is being kept. It should also state that the item will be kept for the duration of the school year or until the parent/guardian retrieves the item.
3. Upon the parent's coming to school and requesting the item, the contraband item may be retrieved. The student's parent or guardian must come to the school and request the return of the item. Any item not requested for return in this way should be disposed of at the end of the school year by the school.

References

Cornfield v. Consolidated High Sch. Dist. No. 230, 991 F.2d 1316 (7th Cir. 1993).

Day, R. (1994). *Legal issues surrounding safe schools.* Topeka, KS: National Organization on Legal Problems of Education.

Dise, J., Iyer, C., & Debler, M. (1994). *Searches of students, lockers and automobiles.* Detroit, MI: Educational Risk, Inc.

Goals 2000: Educate America Act (1994). Public Law 103-227 (20 USC 5812).

New Jersey v. T.L.O. 469 U.S. 325, 340, 105 S. Ct. 733 (1985).

Sorenson, G., Cambron-McCabe, N., & Thomas, S. (1993). Search and seizure in the public schools. In W. Camp, J. Underwood, M. Connelly, & K. Lane (Eds.), *The principal's legal handbook* (pp. 3–12). Topeka, KS: National Organization on Legal Problems of Education.

Vernonia Sch. Dist. 471 v. Acton (U.S. Supreme Court No. 94-590, 1995).

SEXUAL HARASSMENT IN THE SCHOOLS

*R*ecently, we heard someone state that schools are a breeding ground for sexual harassers and sexual abusers. That someone would make such a harsh statement caused us to stop and think about what we as educators are allowing in our schools. Are we condoning behaviors by ignoring them? Are we choosing to laugh off inappropriate sexual comments that males are making to females and vice versa? Are we allowing inappropriate touching in our school hallways? If we are, then perhaps we are promoting sexual harassment and abu e. In a 1993 research study entitled "The Culture of Sexual Harassment in Secondary Schools," reported in a *USA Today* article by T. Henry (1996), the lead researcher, Valerie Lee concluded that U.S. secondary schools have not responded well to the problem of sexual harassment and that the major response of the schools has been to ignore the problem as much as possible.

We have long believed that low-level aggression becomes high-level aggression if ignored. Thus, as we stated earlier, we believe that low-level aggression by students, whether sexual harassment or otherwise, should not be tolerated and must have a consequence. Students cannot think that aggression is appropriate behavior in the school setting. If they believe that such behavior is acceptable, the behavior will escalate. The following is a true story that, sadly, supports the point we are making here. A building principal called one of us (BHJ) to relate something that had just happened in her school. A 12-year-old male student with a learning disability had grabbed a young female student on an inappropriate part of her body. The author (BHJ) provided some advice to the principal, including the recommendation that there should be a clear consequence for the male student. The principal responded to the advice with, "Well, it really wasn't that bad." The principal decided to ignore the behavior, hoping it would go away. Two weeks later, the same young man molested the young lady.

School officials cannot allow behaviors like that of the young boy just described to occur in an environment that should be safe for all children. When such behaviors are ignored and when children are not taught that inappropriate sexual talk or touching is not acceptable, more serious events are more likely to occur.

What Is Sexual Harassment?

Title VII (Section 703) of the Civil Rights Act of 1964 (42 U.S.C. 2000e-2(a)) prohibits discrimination on the basis of sex, race, color, religion, or national origin. The Equal Opportunity Commission, the agency responsible for implementing Title VII, issued guidelines in 1980 (Section 1604.11) for determining what constitutes sexual harassment:

> Unwelcome sexual advances, requests for sexual favors, and other verbal or physical conduct of a sexual nature constitute sexual harassment when (1) submission to such conduct is made either

explicitly or implicitly a term or condition of an individual's employment, (2) submission to or rejection of such conduct by an individual is used as the basis for employment decisions affecting such individual, or (3) such conduct has the purpose or effect of unreasonably interfering with an individual's work performance or creating an intimidating, hostile, or offensive working environment.

Since that time, two forms of sexual harassment have been recognized: *quid pro quo* harassment and *hostile environment* harassment. Quid pro quo harassment can be defined as conduct involving the conditioning of a benefit on the offering of sexual favors ("If you do this for me, I will give this to you"). Hostile environment harassment involves the maintenance of an atmosphere that unreasonably interferes with an individual's performance or creates a hostile or offensive environment. Both types of harassment can occur in schools.

According to Elaine Yaffe (1995), "schools can no longer dismiss the problem as they did in the past, because the law now says that unequal education opportunity results from sexual harassment, and that makes it a form of discrimination. Such behavior denies targets of harassment their full educational opportunities" (p. k2).

Examples of sexual harassment in the schools include whistling, making cat calls, making sexual gestures, teasing and taunting, flipping up a student's skirt, pulling down a student's gym shorts, asking personal, sexually oriented questions, unwelcome touching, leering, staring, namecalling, making unwelcome requests for dates, propositioning, giving sexual gifts, stalking, snapping a student's bra, making off-color jokes, using sexual or sexist language, writing suggestive or sexually explicit letters or notes, drawing personalized graffiti, wearing offensive clothing, grabbing or patting another or one's own personal body parts, displaying pornographic materials, making sexual innuendos, graphically describing girls or boys, rating students' sexual attributes, spreading sexual rumors, intimidation, and rape.

We are reminded of an instance in which school staff allowed students to give "wedgies," an act described as one student yanking up on another student's pants. The general feeling among the staff was that the act was just a game and that it was "cute." Because it was allowed, the behavior became rampant. To our chagrin, when one girl said it bothered her and wanted the behavior to stop, the principal just laughed.

Jansen (1994) reported that sexual harassment is not about sex. Rather, it is about a person's use of power to get what he or she wants. She stressed that the behavior affects bystanders as well as victims. When bystanders view sexual harassment and see nothing done about it, they begin to feel unsafe. If they are students viewing the behavior in school, they may feel that the school and community condone the behavior. But schools, Jansen stated, can be an important part of the solution to the problem in society as a whole, for they are a vehicle for transmitting basic community values.

Bradway (1994) dispelled several myths when she, based on two surveys on sexual harassment of students in schools, reported that sexual harassment usually happens in public view and often with adult witnesses. From one survey conducted by the Wellesley College Center for Research on Women, she noted that 94% of the incidents of harassment took place in classrooms and 76% of the incidents of harassment occurred in the school hallway. Teachers were present one-third of the time. This information was collected from 4,200 female respondents to a survey that appeared in the September, 1992, issue of *Seventeen Magazine* and was reported in 1993 (Stein, Marshall, & Tropp, 1993).

The other poll Bradway cites, *Hostile Hallways* (AAUW, 1993), conducted by Louis B. Harris for the American Association of University Women (AAUW), was based on information from 1,632 students in grades 8 through 11, both male and female, in 79 schools. Of those surveyed, 85% of the girls and 76% of the boys reported having experienced sexual harassment at their school. In addition to shedding light on the depth of the problem, the *Hostile Hallways* results clearly dispel the myth that females are the only students harassed. Almost 80% of the students polled pointed to other students as the harassers.

The same survey revealed the serious educational impact for students who are sexually harassed. Many students who reported having been harassed did not want to go to school, did not want to talk in class, found it hard to pay attention in class, made lower grades on tests, papers or in class than before they were sexually harassed, or found it hard to study.

Legal Issues

Through Title VII of the Civil Rights Act of 1964 as well as through Title IX of the Education Amendments of 1972, the 14th Amendment to the U.S. Constitution, and other human rights acts, U.S. courts have ruled that sexual harassment is discriminatory and unlawful. Recently, the number of court cases that deal with sexual harassment in schools has increased. Those cases have demonstrated varying natures of opinion based on these laws.

The Supreme Court Case of *Franklin v. Gwinnett Pub-*

lic Schools brought the issue of sexual harassment in schools to the forefront. The Court ruled that schools can be held liable for both monetary and compensatory damages that result from a teacher's sexual harassment of a student. According to Shoop and Hayhow (1994), this decision has been interpreted in subsequent cases to mean that schools are liable for all types of sexual harassment, including teacher-student, student-student, and student-teacher.

For example, when ruling on a complaint that involved students sexually harassing other students in an elementary school in Eden Prairie, Minnesota, the Office for Civil Rights found that the school system was in violation of Title IX for "failing to take timely and effective responsive action to address...multiple or severe acts of sexual harassment" (OCR 5-92-1194, 1331 and Appendix). The victims were eight girls, the youngest being a second grader. The girls were subjected to many severe acts of sexual harassment by other students, including offensive sexual references, name-calling, unwelcome touching, intimidation, spitting, and propositions. As part of the settlement with the Office for Civil Rights, the district agreed to develop written guidelines to assist school personnel in taking corrective action when a complaint is made and to monitor the effectiveness of the system.

Zirkel (1995) noted that filing a complaint with the Office for Civil Rights, as was done in Eden Prairie, Minnesota, is one means of obtaining relief, but he cautioned that the remedy is usually limited to a directive to put appropriate policies and procedures in place. State law proceedings, he noted, can offer stronger relief, such as teacher termination or monetary damages, but those results are rare. A more appealing alternative, he wrote, may be to turn to federal legislation and the U.S. Constitution, although even here the results may be varied. He discusses the case of *Doe v. Petaluma City School District,* decided in the Ninth Circuit in 1995. A junior-high student in a California school district was allegedly sexually harassed by both boys and girls throughout seventh and eighth grades. When the student, Jane Doe, reported the problem to the school counselor, the counselor said, "Boys will be boys," and further stated that girls could not be sexually harassed by other girls. The counselor never told her about the Title IX coordinator (the person designated by the school to coordinate the investigation of Title IX complaints) or the grievance procedure. Jane's mother asked for and was granted a transfer for her. Sadly, Jane continued to be harassed in the new school. Her parents moved her again, this time to a private school. Jane suffered medical and psychological problems as a result of the trauma and had to undergo treatment. Jane's parents filed suit for monetary damages on the basis of Title IX of the Education Amendments of 1972. They also claimed that the school district, the principal, and the counselor had violated Jane's liberty, or due-process rights, under the 14th Amendment. The court ruled that the counselor's failure to act occurred prior to the 1992 U.S. Supreme Court decision in *Franklin v. Gwinnett County Public Schools.* Therefore, the counselor, along with the principal and the school district, was entitled to qualified immunity because the law at the time of the incidents did not create a clearcut duty to act.

Some cases, however, have strictly followed the letter of the law in Title IX, which addresses only teacher-student harassment. In *Rowinsky v. Bryan Independent School District,* for example, the Fifth Circuit Court ruled on April 2, 1996, that two sisters in the eighth grade in Bryan, Texas, who stated that they had been tormented throughout the year on the school bus by a boy who grabbed them inappropriately and used foul language, had no claim under Title IX because the harassment was not conducted by school employees. In 1996, the Supreme Court denied the request to hear this case.

With the varying opinions, in legal decisions on student-student sexual harassment, it is likely that the issue will be heard in the Supreme Court. Even without such a decision, however, schools must stop tolerating such behavior if they are to assure a safe, hostility-free environment for students. In the meantime, on August 14, 1996, Norma Cantu, the Assistant Secretary for Civil Rights, wrote a letter to educators clarifying the position of the Office for Civil Rights on schools' responsibility for investigating allegations of sexual harassment of a student or students by another student or group of students that create a hostile environment. She stated that "a school will be liable for the conduct of its students that creates a sexually hostile environment where (i) a hostile environment exists, (ii) the school knows ("has notice") of the harassment, and (iii) the school fails to take immediate and appropriate steps to remedy it" (p. 3).

School officials should also bear in mind that sexual harassment that involves a minor student in a school setting can be considered a criminal offense under laws relating to child abuse. School administrators should make themselves aware of when it is appropriate to include law enforcement in these types of incidents.

Combating the Problem of Sexual Harassment in the Schools

The following step-by-step guidelines are provided to help school staff combat the problem of sexual harassment in the schools.

1. Educators should thoroughly examine their school environment for occurrences of sexual harassment. We recommend direct observation, talking with students and staff, and using questionnaires. Through observation, educators may see that students are making sexually offensive comments to others in the halls and elsewhere. Through talking with both students and staff, educators can learn what their concerns are. Through questionnaires for students, staff, and parents, they can gain a greater awareness of any problems.

2. Schools should establish clear rules and expectations in all areas, including sexual harassment. School, hall, and cafeteria rules should be posted within view of students. The rules should state that sexually inappropriate comments or actions will not be tolerated.

3. Schools must establish policies and procedures for dealing with sexual harassment complaints, incidents, and appeals. A sample sexual harassment policy that schools can adapt for their own use is provided in Appendix F.

4. Schools should establish clear consequences for students and staff who engage in sexual harassment and should delineate those consequences in the school handbook. In addition, the consequences

must be rendered whenever sexual harassment occurs. Strauss (1992) outlined the following possible consequences for incidents of sexual harassment:

a. For the first offense, a verbal warning.

b. For the first or subsequent offenses, a written report entered into the student's file, an apology to the victim (see #9 for further discussion), a fine paid to the county sexual assault program, writing a paper on the topic of sexual harassment, learning more about sexual harassment through classes, reading, and audio-visual programs, a parent-teacher-student conference, police involvement if sexual assault is committed, and community service.

5. Extensive training on what constitutes sexual harassment, on the school policy, and on means of identifying and preventing incidents of sexual harassment should be provided to students and staff. Several curriculums are available that address the issue of sexual harassment. Any curriculum that is adopted should accomplish the following student outcomes:

a. Students will understand the legal definition of sexual harassment.

b. Students will understand the functional definition of sexual harassment.

c. Students will understand the school's policy in this regard.

d. Students will be able to devise solutions to the problem of sexual harassment or appropriate responses to unwelcome or inappropriate sexual advances.

e. Students will have the tools to identify, respond to, and prevent sexual harassment.

   f. Students will understand the impact of sexual harassment on the harasser, the victim, and the entire school community.

For student training, we recommend the following teaching strategies:

   a. All information provided should be framed in a positive and constructive manner.

   b. The information should be free of bias.

   c. The teacher should model appropriate interpersonal behavior.

   d. The teacher should model respect for individual values and beliefs.

   e. Students should be encouraged to express a range of opinions.

   f. Nonsexist terminology and language should be used.

   g. The teacher should use stories and examples to illustrate and highlight information.

The main purposes of staff training programs are to make staff more aware of the issue of sexual harassment in the schools and to teach staff how to provide the training to their students. All school staff need to be aware of the need that exists in all schools today for increased supervision of students, the importance of dealing immediately with inappropriate sexual comments or actions, and the school policy dealing with harassment.

6. Parents should be notified of all procedures the school establishes for dealing with sexual harassment. The notification should explain the school

policy, stress that it is being implemented to assure a safe environment for all students, and encourage parents to report to the school administration any instances of sexual harassment they learn about from their children. At times, students who are afraid to report an incident at school may tell their parents about it. Students and their parents need to know that it is okay to report any incident and, in fact, that the school encourages them to do so.

7. Each reported incident should be thoroughly investigated and the investigation documented. Schools should take every report of sexual harassment seriously. A sample sexual harassment incident report form and a form for documenting the decision of an appeals panel (when an appeals hearing has been held) are included in Appendix F.

8. Schools must comply with state procedures for criminal activity that constitutes sexual abuse, such as sexual assault. Definitions of criminal sexual assault and criminal sexual abuse can be found in each state's criminal code. Whenever an incident involves such an offense, the police and the state agency that investigates child abuse must be notified.

9. Schools should consider using the following techniques when dealing with incidents of sexual harassment:

   a. Conflict resolution, which helps the victim and perpetrator come to closure concerning the incident.

   b. Having the victim write a letter about his or her feelings to the perpetrator.

c. Having the perpetrator apologize to the victim. We have found that requiring students to face their victims and apologize for their behavior helps them to confront reality. We use this technique in addition to rendering other consequences. An important aspect of the technique is teaching the student the process of making an apology, that is, (1) to state specifically what he or she did, (2) to state that he or she apologizes, (3) to state what he or she will do in similar situations in the future, and (4) to state the apology using an appropriate voice tone, making eye contact, and exhibiting an appropriate stance.

10. Schools should post sexual harassment notices, such as the one shown in Figure 9.1, throughout all school buildings.

**HAPPY DAYS SCHOOL
PROHIBITS
SEXUAL HARASSMENT**

Sexual harassment is a form of discrimination prohibited by Title IX of the Education Amendments of 1972.

Sexual harassment is any unwanted attention of a sexual nature.

Incidents of sexual harassment should be reported to the principal or assistant principal.

 Figure 9.1   Sample Sexual Harassment Notice

In summary, school personnel must provide an environment in which sexual harassment is not tolerated. Complaints of sexual harassment must be taken seriously and investigated in a timely, thorough, and fair manner. When the aforementioned steps are followed consistently, a message is clearly sent that sexual harassment will not be tolerated.

References

The American Association of University Women (AAUW) Educational Foundation. (1993). *Hostile Hallways: The AAUW survey on sexual harassment in America's schools.* Washington, DC: Louis Harris and Associates.

Bradway, B. (1994). Sexual harassment in schools. *School Intervention Report, 7*(4), 1–12.

Cantu, N. (1996). *Sexual harassment guidance: Peer harassment.* Washington, DC: United States Department of Education, Office for Civil Rights.

Doe v. Petaluma City Sch. Dist. (9th Cir. No. 94-15917, 1995).

Equal Employment Opportunity Commission Guidelines on Sexual Harassment. (29 C.F.R. Section 1604.11{A}) effective November 10, 1980.

Franklin v. Gwinnett County Public Schools, 112 S.Ct. 1028 (1992).

Henry, T. (1996, July 23). Sexual harassment pervades schools, study says. *USA Today,* p. 8B.

Jansen, G. (1994). Sexual harassment in the schools. Unpublished handout given on June 24, 1994, to participants in the Illinois Institute for Dispute Resolution conference. Available from Golie Jansen, Eastern Washington University, Spokane, Washington.

Lee, V. (1993). *The culture of sexual harassment in secondary schools.* Research study. Ann Arbor: University of Michigan.

Office for Civil Rights (OCR) 5-92-1194, 11331 and Appendix.

Rowinsky v. Bryan Independent School District (80 F. 3d, 1006 5th Circuit 17 S. Ct. 165, 1996) (*cert denied* 1996).

Shoop, R., & Hayhow, J. (1994). *Sexual harassment in our schools.* Boston: Allyn and Bacon.

Stein, N., Marshall, N., & Tropp, L. (1993). *Secrets in public: Sexual harassment in our schools*. A report on the results of a *Seventeen Magazine* survey. Wellesley, MA: Wellesley College Center for Research on Women.

Strauss, S. (1992). *Sexual harassment and teens*. Minneapolis: Free Spirit Publishing.

Title VII of the 1964 Civil Rights Act (42 USC 2000e et seq.).

Yaffe, E. (1995). Expensive, illegal, and wrong: Sexual harassment in our schools. Kappan special report. *Phi Delta Kappan, 77*(3), k1–k15.

Zirkel, P. (1995). Student-to-student sexual harassment. *The Kappan, 76*(8), 648–649.

SEXUAL PERPETRATORS IN THE SCHOOLS

*A*n increasing number of students within U.S. schools have previous convictions for inappropriate sexual acts or have been accused in the past of making inappropriate sexual contacts but were not prosecuted. Little has been written on the topic of sexual perpetrators in the schools; most likely it has been assumed that these children are in treatment facilities or incarcerated.

When attempting to conduct a literature search on what educators need to know when working with this population of students within the public schools, one of us (BHJ) was informed by a librarian that nothing on the topic was available. "These children are in institutions," the librarian said. However, that is not always the case. Some children who have been convicted of sexual crimes have moved with their families to another state, where they are now attending school. Others who have been found guilty of criminal sexual activity and put on probation are also attending schools. Many families who have been ordered to seek outpatient treatment for their children have chosen not to do so, instead moving the family in the hope that no one will learn of their child's past conviction. In one such case, the parents moved from the state where their 13-year-old had been convicted, but school officials in the new community learned of the conviction. The family then moved to another community, but again the new school received the information. The probation officer was able to contact the student's previous probation officer, who confirmed the information and agreed to attend a staffing on the student (the student was in special education). Based on the information that individual provided, school officials were able to plan an appropriate placement for the student in a structure that provided continuous supervision. In our work, we have found that many school officials and family service agency officials know very little about criminal sexual activity in children. One family service official commented that no child would hurt another child his own age. Another stated, "There is no reason to worry. This boy only molests infants."

Overview of the Problem

Barbaree and Cortoni (1993) reported that a substantial proportion of all sex offenses can be attributed to adolescents. Indeed, according to their figures, 20% of all rapes and as many as 50% of all assaults against children are committed by juveniles. Likewise, Barbaree and Cortoni (1993) report that professionals who work with adult sex offenders have reported that 50% of their clients indicate that their sexually deviant behavior began in adolescence. These professionals have also reported that juvenile offenders and their families are likely to deny the offense or minimize it. Often, they make excuses or blame the victim. Adolescent sex offenses have in the past been viewed by some counselors as simply being sexual experimentation and a part of normal development. Unfortunately, this view just reinforces the offenders' behavior. Similarly, today's view and treatment of juvenile sexual offenders as noncriminals encourages the offenders and their families in their denial and minimization (Barbaree & Cortoni, 1993).

The problem is not just with adolescents and adults. Gray and Pithers (1993) reported that the onset of sexually abusive behaviors can precede adolescence. They noted that in Vermont, between 1984 and 1989, 200 children under 10 years of age were discovered to have sexually abused others, and that number included only children who had committed forceful or repetitive acts.

The National Adolescent Perpetrator Network, which as of 1988 had created over 520 programs specifically designed to treat juvenile sex offenders, contends that the primary objective of intervention with these offenders is protection of the community. When the security and treatment needs of these offenders are in conflict with the needs of victims, the needs of the victims and community should be given the highest priority.

We agree and feel that the same philosophy must exist among school officials. The needs of nonoffenders, the majority of the school population, for a safe learning environment must be given the highest priority.

Marquoit and Dobbins (1995) cautioned that it is the responsibility of educators to develop treatment approaches for sexual offenders that serve the best interests of the rest of the children and therefore, in turn, help to ensure the safety of the community. They further advised educators working with sexual perpetrators in school to be cautious that they do not use highly punitive and dehumanizing approaches. While taking measures to protect the other students, they must also treat the perpetrator with respect. According to these authors, "The safety of the community is best served when the therapeutic focus is on developing a self-confident, caring human being" (p. 33). Educators must treat all students with respect and care.

Margolin (1983) reported that confidentiality cannot apply in the treatment of this population because it promotes the secrecy that supports the offenses, feeding into the offenders' denial and minimization. School officials are put in the position of balancing the confidentiality laws that govern students versus providing necessary information to those who work with the student so that other students will be protected. For example, the teacher who works with the student must have the information so that he or she can provide additional supervision of the student. If the student requires intervention by any other staff member, that staff member has a right to know the information in order to implement any specific plan. Certainly, school officials cannot downplay such information and must take all necessary precautions to protect the other schoolchildren. Further, school officials must work with all other agencies involved in overseeing the behavior of juvenile offenders to ensure that treatment plans are sex-offender specific. Treatment that is non-sex-offender specific is not sufficient to modify sexually abusive behaviors (Barbaree & Cortoni, 1993).

Characteristics of Children Who Are Sexual Perpetrators

Johnson (1991) made the following points about children who are sexual perpetrators:

1. They seek out children whom they can force, fool, or bribe into sexual activity with them.
2. They often use threats to keep their victims from telling others about what they have done.
3. They engage in coercive sexual behaviors with older, younger, or same-age children. Some molest infants.
4. They will continue to engage in these behaviors even after harsh punishment. Their behavior will not abate without significant and prolonged intervention.
5. They almost always have behavioral problems at home and at school and have few friends.
6. 25% are female.
7. 60% to 70% of male child perpetrators had been sexually abused in the past.

School Procedures

Taking these points—and the important responsibility of educators to assure a safe school for all students—into account, we recommend the following procedures for working with schoolchildren who are sexual perpetrators.

1. Whenever an educator hears information about previous sexual offenses of a student, that educator has a responsibility to verify the accuracy of the information, document it, and note its source. The source may be, for example, "records from the probation department," "verified school records," or "caseworker X from the Department of Children and Family Services." Obviously, school officials should never operate on hearsay or second- or third-hand information.

2. After documenting the information, the educator should share the information that is critical in supervising the student with all school personnel who work with the student, stressing its confidentiality. For example, teachers would need to know that a student has a history of problems occurring in the restroom and thus should not be allowed to go to the restroom at the same time as other students.

3. The student should be supervised at all times. Many students with a history of sexual offenses will be best accommodated in small school settings or self-contained settings in which there is continual supervision. If such students are to be accommodated in a large school setting, hallway and cafeteria times must be supervised.

4. The student should not be allowed to go to the restroom with any other student. Teachers should be discrete and not single out the student as being the only one in the class who is unable to go to the restroom at the same time as the others. A suggestion is to give the child a task to perform while the others go to the restroom and permit the child to go later. In some small special school settings, it is common practice to have all students go to the restroom one at a time with an adult standing outside the door. Teachers probably will need to have an assistant who can walk to the restroom with the student and check to see if the restroom is vacant before allowing the student to enter the restroom. In many schools, students are allowed to go the restroom throughout the day so it is necessary to assure that the room is vacant before allowing the student to use the facility.

5. If the student rides a school bus, he or she must be assigned a seat as close to the driver as possible and should not be allowed to share the seat with any other student. Another option is to consider individual transportation for the student.

   More and more problems are occurring on school buses. Drivers are expected to supervise and discipline an entire group of students while facing away from them. To make matters worse, they are often not well trained in behavior management techniques. School officials must work with drivers to plan effective behavior management strategies. We recommend assigned seats for all students, a measure that would, in itself, ensure that perpetrators are not singled out.

   School officials may also want to assign an adult bus monitor to sit with the identified student. We do not recommend that perpetrators be assigned to buses with high-back seats, where the driver and the video camera, if the bus has one, cannot catch what is going on during the bus ride, unless the student is in the front seat.

6. School staff must observe the student closely in the cafeteria and other settings, watching for such subtle behaviors as brushing against someone or hand-touching under the table. By engaging in such subtle behaviors, students minimize their chances of getting caught yet still intimidate other children. The behaviors can be so subtle that they are hard to detect unless close supervision is occurring.

7. Any observed sexual touching by a student must be investigated by school personnel in accordance with school policy and must be reported to the lo-

cal police and the state agency that investigates cases of child abuse. The incident should also be reported to the parents of both the perpetrator and the victim and documented in writing for the student perpetrator's file. The incident should also be documented in the victim's file. In either file the name of the other student involved should be omitted, for confidentiality reasons.

8. Any inappropriate sexual talk heard by or reported to school personnel should be thoroughly investigated in accordance with the school's sexual harassment policy (see Chapter 9).

9. All students in the school should be informed that inappropriate sexual activity is not acceptable in the school setting and will not be tolerated.

10. School officials should work closely with any student who has a history of sexual offenses and his or her family to facilitate sessions with the appropriate community agency and let them know the community resources that are available. In addition, a school social worker should work with the student, encouraging the student to discuss his or her feelings. (Often, a sexual perpetrator may not feel that he or she is able to control the impulse to make sexual contact; it is imperative that such students have someone to talk with about their feelings.)

11. At the same time that the precautions stated herein should be taken, school staff should be sure to treat students with a history of sexual offenses, as well as all other students, with respect and show that they truly care about them. No student's history or problems should ever be discussed within range

of another student's hearing. Further, the student with a history of sexual offenses must receive positive reinforcement when he or she acts appropriately. Staff members must remember that such students are individuals who need treatment and have the right to be treated with respect.

12. If the student with a history of sexual offenses is involved in special education, all of the procedures that are to be implemented must be included as part of the student's behavior management plan in his or her Individualized Education Program.

A sample behavior management plan for a student in special education who has been identified as a sexual perpetrator follows:

1. Billy will stay in the area assigned by the adult in charge and leave that area only after he has received permission from the adult. When leaving the area, he shall be escorted by the adult. If Billy leaves an area without permission, he will receive a point fine on his point card. If Billy leaves an area without permission twice in a day, he will receive a major infraction, resulting in the loss of all of his special privileges.

2. Billy will receive a positive point on his point card for every 20 minutes that he follows teaching directions.

3. Billy will go to the restroom at a different time than other students in his class and will only use the restroom when no one else is in it.

4. In classroom areas where all students sit together as a group, Billy will have an assigned seat next to an adult.

5. Billy will not be allowed to move to different areas of the building without supervision.
6. On the bus, Billy will sit alone in the front seat.
7. Any report of Billy sexually touching another student will be immediately investigated by school officials in accordance with school policy. The incident will also be reported to the police department and the Department of Children and Family Services for investigation. Such behavior will result in a major infraction.
8. Any report of Billy making inappropriate sexual talk will be thoroughly investigated in accordance with the school's sexual harassment procedure. If the accusation is found to be true, Billy will be told that such behavior is not acceptable in the school setting and will receive a point fine on his point card.
9. The social worker will be on call to talk with Billy whenever Billy feels that he cannot control his impulse to make sexual contact. The social worker will also work with Billy's family to facilitate counseling by the appropriate mental agency.

References

Barbaree, H., & Cortoni, F. (1993). Treatment of the juvenile sex offender within the criminal justice and mental health systems. In H. Barbaree, W. Marshall, & S. Hudson (Eds.), *The juvenile sex offender* (pp. 243–262). New York: Guilford Press.

Gray, A., & Pithers, W. (1993). Relapse prevention with sexually aggressive adolescents and children: Expanding treatment and supervision. In H. Barbaree, W. Marshall, & S. Hudson (Eds.), *The juvenile sex offender* (pp. 289–317). New York: Guilford Press.

Johnson, T. (1991, Fall). Children who molest children. *The APSAC Advisor,* pp. 9–11, 23.

Margolin, L. (1983). A treatment model for the adolescent sex offender. *Journal of Offender Counseling, Services and Rehabilitation, 8,* 1–12.

Marquoit, J., & Dobbins, M. (1995). Do juvenile sexual offenders have strengths? *Journal of Emotional and Behavioral Problems, 4*(2), 31–33.

GANG PREVENTION AND INTERVENTION

*G*ang activity is a major problem in today's schools. In addition to posing a great threat to school safety, youth gangs are using the schools as a recruiting ground for new members. According to Ronald Stephens (1993, p. 219), "Youth gangs, whose organization and existence at one time had primarily a social basis, now are motivated by violence, extortion, intimidation, and illegal trafficking in drugs and weapons." Indeed, youth gangs are commonly defined as organized groups of adolescents involved in criminal activity. When school officials are unaware or choose to deny that gang problems may exist in their schools, they are, in reality, allowing students to sell drugs at school, intimidate other students so much that children are afraid to go to school, extort fees from other students to obtain protection, or stake out parts of the school as their own turf. Such school officials are allowing school safety to be badly compromised.

The danger posed by gangs has received a great deal of media attention, but the other aspect of the problem—the fact that gangs are using schools as recruiting grounds—is equally important. Everyone wants to belong, and children who are attempting to belong somewhere are easy targets for gang recruitment. Sadly, they do not realize that once they get into a gang, quitting is rarely an option. Other children join gangs to gain a sense of identity. And students who feel unsafe sometimes join a gang in order to be protected.

Warning Signs of Potential Gang Involvement

Educators need to be alert to the following warning signs that a student may have become involved in a gang. The presence of any of these signs should be cause for concern and investigation.

- A sudden drop in academic performance that cannot be explained by a particular reason such as illness or changes at home
- Detachment from school activities—the student was previously involved in extracurricular activities but has now lost interest; the student previously talked openly with staff members but now refuses to do so
- Use of a nickname that has questionable meaning—for example, a student is called "Fat Daddy" though school officials had not heard him called that before
- Symbolic drawings made on books, papers, or self—some include six-pointed stars, the initials "GD," bunny heads, and pitchforks
- Changes in clothing—the student starts wearing particular colors or a hat tilted to the left or right; the student starts wearing all new clothes that are very expensive; the student may start "sagging" his pants; the student may start wearing excessive amounts of jewelry

- Changes in friends—a student who previously was a loner or had a particular group of friends is now frequently seen socializing with other students or with a completely different group of students than before
- Adoption of an attitude of rebelliousness and resistance toward school and parents—the student had previously followed school rules but now questions and breaks many of those rules; the student becomes reclusive at home, at school, or both
- Signs of drug or alcohol use or abuse
- Sudden increase in money—a student comes to school with large wads of money when previously he or she had none or very little
- Decrease in school attendance—a student who previously had good school attendance starts skipping school

Although any one of these signs may not alone indicate gang involvement, its presence should provide a warning to school personnel that further investigation is warranted.

Recruitment of Young Children into Gangs

Schools can no longer assume that gang activity is limited to students in middle and high schools. We are aware of 7-year-old students who were recruited into gangs. Young children have a unique appeal to gangs: They can commit crimes for the gang but if caught will not receive a stiff legal penalty because of their age. We also know of a 9-year-old student who, while being evaluated for special education by a school psychologist, drew pictures that clearly contained several gang signs.

Schools also can no longer assume that gang activity is limited to big cities or large schools. Both in small schools and schools in small communities we have observed gang graffiti in the restrooms, students drawing gang symbols in art class, and students wearing clothing depicting gang signs.

Steps to Combat Gang Activity in Schools

We recommend the following step-by-step procedures for combating gang activity in schools.

1. All school officials must admit that their school has a gang problem or the potential for a gang problem. If officials deny that a gang problem or a potential gang problem exists, students may perceive them as ignorant, and gangs can take over the school before school officials are aware of what is happening. Huff (1989) reported that denial by school officials of gang problems or gang activity appears to facilitate victimization by the gangs, especially in public schools. In his study of schools in three of Ohio's largest cities, he found that school principals were reluctant to acknowledge gang-related assaults for fear that such problems would be interpreted as negative reflections on their management abilities. According to Huff, their reluctance appeared to encourage gang-related assaults because gang members believed they could operate without consequences for their behavior.
2. Schools must adopt a no-tolerance approach to gang activity. Students must know that their school will not tolerate gang activity of any type on school

grounds, on school buses, or at any school events. Schools must be seen by all students as neutral territory. (Note that by "no-tolerance" we do not mean that students who engage in gang activity should be suspended or expelled from school. As explained later in these guidelines, other consequences are, we feel, more effective in combating the problem.)

3. Schools should work cooperatively with other community agencies, sending representatives to regularly scheduled meetings where information about gang activity in the school and community can be shared. In our local area, school officials meet monthly with members of the police department, the state's attorney's office, and the probation department to discuss gang activity occurring on the streets and in the schools.

4. Schools must notify students, parents, and staff of the policies and procedures established for combating gang activity. All such policies and procedures must also be included in the student handbook. We recommend holding a whole-school assembly at the beginning of the school year in which school officials review the school's expectations with regard to gang and other behavior. We also recommend letting students and their parents know that school officials are networking with the police.

5. Any gang graffiti spotted in the school, on school grounds, or in the general area of the school should be removed at once. As mentioned previously, we recommend that checks of the school building be done both before and after school to, among other things, locate any gang graffiti. Whenever they can

be identified, the students responsible for graffiti should be required to clean it up.

6. Students should be warned that if they are observed making gang-identifiable drawings or having such drawings in their notebooks or other books, the material will be confiscated, dated, identified, and forwarded to the local police department. A copy of the material, so dated and identified, will be placed in the student's temporary record and shown to the student's parents. We have found that telling students that any drawings will be confiscated and immediately turned over to the police has helped to curtail such activity.

   We recommend that periodic in-service training for staff be held at which members of the local police department educate the staff on recent gang signs and symbols. Specific procedures for dealing with gang drawings and gang graffiti are listed in Figure 11.1.

7. Schools should include in their dress code a prohibition against wearing gang attire (see Chapter 7). Because clothing is a primary form of gang identification, gang attire must be discussed in the school dress code. It is important to remember that, in establishing a dress code, great care must be taken to maintain the balance between student's First Amendment right of free expression and the school's responsibility to provide a safe educational environment (Stephens, 1993).

8. Any crime, including gang-related crimes committed in a school or on school grounds should be handled as a crime. Educators are not doing students a favor when they allow them to commit

1. Explain to all students that gang drawings and gang graffiti will not be tolerated in any form in or around the school.
2. Develop a working agreement with the local police whereby the school will report and provide to the police any gang drawings that are brought to school or drawn at school. Make students aware of the agreement. Explain that the school networks with the police and will provide the police with all gang drawings and with names of individuals who make such drawings or exhibit gang affiliation.
3. Request that the police provide school staff with in-service training on the identification and recognition of gang graffiti, gang symbols, and gang attire.
4. Confiscate and document any signs of gang representation that occur in the school. Photograph or photocopy confiscated items. Turn originals over to the police.
5. Immediately remove any gang graffiti or drawings.
6. Should a student show any signs of gang membership immediately notify the student's parents. Document the discussion with the parents and place the documentation in the student's temporary file.
7. Establish a dress code that specifically designates gang attire as unacceptable in the school. A provision of the dress code should specify that tattoos showing explicit gang representation must be covered at all times.

 Figure 11.1 Procedures for Dealing with Gang Graffiti and Gang Drawings

crimes at school. Such tolerance will only encourage the behavior, both in school and on the streets. Educators must teach students, at an early age, that a crime is a crime, wherever it is committed. Should a student commit a crime at school, we recommend that the school press charges on behalf of the school rather than placing the onus on the student victim to press the charges. By doing so, schools will prevent the possibility of perpetrators intimidating victims to force them to drop the charges. However, as discussed earlier, we feel that schools should press charges only when there is an adult witness to the crime.

9. Schools must set high expectations for all students in the areas of student behavior, academic performance, and school attendance.

Clear rules and expectations must be established for what behaviors are allowed at school and what behaviors are not allowed. Students who follow the rules should be recognized for doing so; students who do not follow the rules should be rendered logical and immediate consequences. We encourage educators to expect good behavior from all students; even those students who are involved in gang activity away from school should be expected to behave in school. If teachers show students that they believe they can make wise decisions, they will likely do so.

Also noted, such caring will help increase teacher safety as well as student safety. According to Huff (1989), teachers who demonstrate that they care about students and are firm but fair in their expectations are rarely, if ever, the victims of assault by gang members. His research showed that it is those teachers who do not follow through, who back down, and who are easily intimidated who are more likely to be the victims of assault. Huff also noted that overly aggressive behavior directed at gang members appears to backfire.

With regard to academics, Huff's research showed that teachers who insist on academic performance, within the context of a caring relationship are unlikely to be assaulted. In fact, not a single gang member he studied knew of such a teacher who had been assaulted. His research provides yet another reason for teachers to show their students that they believe in them and know they can do the academic tasks expected of them. Rutter, Maughan, Mortimore, Ouston, and Smith (1982) found that there was an inverse relationship between, on one hand, the amount of academic work students had to do and the amount of educational material on display in a school and, on the other hand, the amount of graffiti observed in the school. His findings contest the belief held by many school officials that any material displayed in schools—pupils' work, pictures, or posters—will become quickly damaged or defaced. Indeed, Rutter's findings suggest that visual displays of various kinds are positively related to positive outcomes. In our work, we have found that students, even at the high-school level, want to have their work and any special accomplishments displayed.

Finally, with regard to school attendance, educators must stress to students that they expect a high level of attendance and believe that the students will come to school. At the same time, they must make school an inviting, caring environment so that students will want to attend. Further discussion on creating a caring school environment was provided in Chapter 3.

10. Schools must provide more supervision than in the past both within and outside the school setting. Problem behavior has been found to be especially high during unstructured periods of time, such as when students are passing in the hallway between classes. We recommend utilizing additional hall monitors. Teaching staff, for example, can be asked to step into the doorways during passing times as well as before and after school. Other effective options are to install video equipment in the hallways and to stagger passing times so that fewer students are in the halls at the same time.

    Bus stops are another area at which problems frequently occur. If problems have been reported at a given bus stop, school officials may want to ask the police to patrol that area. Some schools have provided additional supervisors for problem bus stops.

    Restrooms, too, should be monitored. One measure taken by some schools is to lock restroom doors during times when all students are supposed to be in class. Restrooms should always be checked before and after use by a group of students. Further, if a problem has been reported with a specific student in the restroom, that student should not be allowed, for a period of time, to go to the restroom when other students are using it.

11. Schools may wish to establish, in cooperation with law enforcement officials, an anonymous gang reporting hot line. As Stephens (1993) reported, students have excellent gang intelligence information to offer. If students know that there is an easy and safe way for them to report gang crimes, they will be more likely to report them.

12. School officials must establish a school environment that makes all students feel welcome and provides all students with a sense of belonging. Students often join gangs because of the sense of belonging they provide. Why can't schools provide that feeling? Figure 11.2 contains a checklist that educators can use to assess the adequacy of their school's response to students' need for belonging. Schools that are clean and nicely decorated will give students a sense that school is a pleasant place to be. We recommend that teachers have students assist in decorating and cleaning their school. By doing so, the students will gain a sense of pride and ownership in the school. One teacher we know had a large round table in her classroom that had a tablecloth on it. Many of her students wanted to do their work at that table. The story reminds us of how people usually collect in the kitchen at home.

The school environment must also be one that accents positive student behavior. That can be accomplished in many ways. One is to give students opportunities to work in community service programs. Not only will they learn the value of helping others, but they will feel a sense of pride.

13. Schools must establish a system of responsibility-based discipline, where students are taught that they

Does your school . . .	Yes	No
Have a positive image?		
Promote school pride in its students?		
Advocate that staff exhibit caring and trust in all students?		
Provide easy student access to teachers and administrators?		
Promote learning that is relevant to future needs?		
Have programs in place for at-risk students?		
Have clearly stated goals?		
Evaluate its goals on an annual basis?		
Have an understandable and usable guidebook for students and parents?		
Have an understandable and usable guidebook for staff?		
Have procedures in place for dealing with criminal activity?		
Have procedures in place for rewarding good attendance and dealing with truancy?		
Encourage students to take responsibility for their actions?		
Administer discipline in a firm, fair, and consistent manner?		
Administer discipline that "teaches" appropriate behaviors?		
Render logical consequences when disciplinary action is necessary?		
Promote alternatives to suspension and expulsion?		
Promote a sense of safety throughout the school building and grounds?		
Promote parent participation and involvement in the educational process?		

 Figure 11.2 Checklist for Assessing How Well a School Is Responding to Its Students' Need for Belonging

are responsible for their own behavior and must deal with the consequences of their behavior in a logical manner. We recommend that schools implement a system of conflict resolution, where students must face others with whom they have had a conflict and arrive at their own solutions to their problems. Haberman and Dill (cited in Bracey, 1995) explored the conditions that children face outside of school, how those conditions affect the children at school, and how schools can be effective in alleviating some of the problems. From their findings, they derived a number of principles for educators to follow for counteracting school violence. One of the principles they cited was for educators to teach children to work through their problems. They stressed, as we do, that a system that uses only enforcement and control and emphasizes punishments will not solve problems. Teachers and school staff must model mediation and conflict resolution techniques every day. Educators cannot assume that students enter school already adept at the forms of communication that facilitate conflict resolution.

We believe that suspension and expulsion should not be the primary discipline techniques at any school. Suspension and expulsion send a clear message to students that they are not wanted in the school and allow students to escape from their problems. For students who do not want to go to school in the first place, suspension and expulsion actually serve as rewards for inappropriate behavior. Alternatives to suspension are discussed in detail in Johns, Carr, and Hoots (1995).

We also believe that students should be given opportunities to be involved in decision making at their school. Such involvement helps students feel valued and provides them with a sense of responsibility. Through student forums and other venues at which students are provided an opportunity to be heard, students will gain a sense of responsibility for the welfare of their school.

14. Training should be provided to all staff on gang identification and intervention. Local law enforcement agencies can teach staff about gang signs and gang clothing in their area. In one school district that we know of, teachers were offered board credit for taking a course on gang identification taught by members of the police department. Teachers need to be knowledgeable about gang signs if they are to take a "no-tolerance" approach to gang activity. Armed with up-to-date information, teachers will be able to recognize any gang signs in their classroom, mark the signs, date them, and turn them over to the school administrator, who would then turn them over to the police.

15. Parents should also receive training about gangs and the signs that may indicate gang involvement. They need to know what changes to look for in their child's behavior. Again, the police department is an excellent resource for providing this training.

In summary, school personnel should respond to any report of student gang action. Although we believe that school personnel should not be judgmental about what students do away from school, we feel strongly that educators must stress to students that gang activity is not appropriate, and will not be tolerated, in the school setting. School personnel must stress the importance of having a safe school for all students.

# References

Bracey, G. (1995). Research: Curbing teen violence. *Phi Delta Kappan, 77*(2), 185–186.

Huff, C. R. (1989). Youth gangs and public policy. *Crime and Delinquency, 35*(4), 530–531.

Johns, B., Carr, V., & Hoots, C. (1995). *Reduction of school violence: Alternatives to suspension.* Horsham, PA: LRP Publications.

Rutter, M., Maughan, B., Mortimore, P., & Ouston, J., with Smith, A. (1982). *Fifteen thousand hours.* Cambridge, MA: Harvard University Press.

Stephens, R. (1993). School-based interventions: Safety and security. In A. Goldstein & C. R. Huff (Eds.), *The gang intervention handbook* (pp. 219–256). Champaign, IL: Research Press.

12

INTERVENTION PROCEDURES FOR TRAUMATIC CRISES

*T*he school community, like any other close-knit community, is seriously affected by the death of any of its members as well as by other major crises, such as an attempted suicide or a serious accident or illness. As stated by Watson, Poda, Miller, Rice, and West (1990), schools must have in place plans for the management of events that cannot be predicted. We believe that such guidelines must be developed not only for humanistic reasons but also to ensure that a rational, tempered atmosphere will prevail when traumatic crises occur.

In this chapter we provide general guidelines for dealing with traumatic crises in schools and specific guidelines to follow in the event of the death of a student or staff member or the potential death of a student. In Chapter 13, we provide information on managing crises that affect school security.

Developing and Implementing a Basic Crisis Plan

Throughout this book, we have stressed the importance of being prepared for situations that may occur. Unpredictable crises are no exception: A crisis plan is a must.

We are not suggesting that schools develop 300-page manuals that cover every possible type of disaster—no one would read them—but we do advocate the development of a basic disaster plan. The following is a step-by-step guideline for developing such a plan.

1. School officials should conduct periodic inventories of the potential for a disaster to occur in their school. For example, do any students or staff have serious illnesses? Is there a feeling of unrest among any group(s) of students?

2. Schools should review what other schools have done when crises have occurred. Educators can learn from both the mistakes and successes of other schools.

3. When developing policies and procedures for dealing with crises, school officials should seek assistance from the local police department. (All of the procedures provided in this book were developed jointly by the police department and the school.) They should also seek input from all other agencies that would be impacted by the procedures.

4. All crisis policies and procedures should specify the following:

   a. Who will serve as the school's spokesperson if this type of crisis occurs? According to St. John (1986), a single spokesperson should be designated to speak for the school. If more than one spokesperson is designated, there is the possibility that contradictory statements may be made.

   The spokesperson will also be the individual who talks to the press. As Jay (1989) discussed, responding to the media with "No comment" will encourage the media to get the story from other, far less reliable sources. The school spokesperson should stick to the facts and give the media as much information as has been verified. If a specific timeline exists for investigating the situation, he or she should let the media know that timeline.

b. Who will serve on a crisis intervention team?
c. What communication system will be used to alert students and staff of the crisis?
d. What special equipment will be needed for dealing with the crisis?
e. Who will tell the staff and who will tell the students (individual teachers, social workers, psychologists)?
f. Who will contact the students' parents?
g. Who will provide support and counseling to students and staff?
h. Who will determine whether any changes will need to be made in the school schedule?
i. Who will subsequently evaluate the process?

5. Once policies and procedures have been developed, they must be disseminated and explained to all personnel who would be impacted. Periodic reviews of the policies and procedures must be made.

6. Schools may wish, as St. John (1986) suggested, to index the crisis plan and place the plan and index in a loose-leaf binder. St. John recommended that the school administrator keep an outline of the crisis plan and all relevant phone numbers on a card in his or her wallet so they are always readily available.

7. Following any traumatic crisis, the school should, within a timely framework, assess the potential impact of the event on all parties involved and arrange appropriate follow-through to provide those parties with closure on the event. Jay (1989) noted the following three actions that the school should take after the immediate crisis is over:
   a. Those who provided extra assistance, were courageous, and were patient throughout the crisis should be thanked.
   b. Efforts should be made to help heal any wounds that remain after the crisis, to help allay any fears that may follow an accident, and to acknowledge the sadness that occurs after a loss.
   c. The crisis team should consider what they could do better next time.

We cannot stress enough the importance of having a crisis plan in place. Few people will be level-headed enough to create such a plan "on the spot" when a crisis occurs. We are reminded of a sad event that occurred in the school at which one of us works. A dedicated and committed teacher was stricken with cancer. For five years, she continued to teach her class of students with severe behavioral disorders. When her illness became very serious, she was hospitalized and spent the last two weeks of her life in the hospital. Many of the staff and students had watched her brave effort to fight the illness and admired her courage. All of her students, some of whom had been in her class for three years, were devastated by her death, and the staff members were in a state of shock and sadness. All of the staff were grateful that the school had a plan in place for dealing with such sad events. No one was in any condition to create such a plan "on the spot."

In another incident that affected the staff and students in one of our schools this year, a young student was beaten, almost to death, by an older man on a weekend. On Monday, school personnel had to notify the staff and talk with the students. Many of the children were afraid that the same thing might happen to them. Counseling had to be made available to the students.

When dealing with any crisis, school personnel should always:

1. Stay calm.
2. Tell the truth.
3. Be as precise as possible.
4. Provide facts to the media. (We recommend that school personnel work with the press; remember, they will always have the last word.)
5. Follow the school's policies and procedures.

What to Do in the Event of the Death of a Student or Staff Member

The following outline details a sample action plan that a school may want to use in the event of the death of a student or staff member.

I. Foster Understanding
A. The school administrator or designee notifies the crisis intervention team.
1. **When?** The team should be called together whenever a student or staff member dies. The team should meet immediately, either during the school day or, if the crisis occurs outside of school hours, at 7:00 a.m.

the following day, having been contacted at home by the principal. That meeting should be immediately followed by a full staff meeting to update staff, answer concerns, and outline the specific process to be followed.

2. **Who/What?** The members of the team and their roles follow:

  a. School administrator or designee—chairs the team; formalizes or oversees its functioning; ensures that the team carries out its agenda.

  b. School administrator or designee—directs staff on actions to be taken, contacts bereaved family for information about assistance needed, and funeral arrangements.

  c. School administrator or designee—supervises and coordinates necessary activities that occur in school.

  d. Psychologist and social worker—coordinate their roles and responsibilities.

  e. School administrator or designee—contacts the press; contacts students' parents (e.g., sending a letter or memo or calling parents).

  f. Teacher and alternate, selected by school administrator—serve as liaison with faculty.

  g. Floating member, selected by school administrator—provides information to other team members on individual who has died, including his or her friends, enemies, etc.

B. The school administrator or other appropriate staff member contacts the family of the person who has died (this should be done before team meets, if possible) to:
  1. Verify information and facts surrounding the crisis.
  2. See how the family defines or understands the crisis (e.g., accident, illness, suicide).
  3. See what the family's wishes are, if any, with regard to sharing information about funeral arrangements, etc., with students and staff.
  4. Briefly outline the general process the school plans to follow.
C. School administrator or designee on crisis intervention team notifies faculty of the death. Also:
  1. Identifies faculty who may be the most vulnerable to the crisis and provides support if necessary.
  2. Prepares a paragraph to give to faculty members to *read to their classes* providing the true facts and briefly explaining what will happen next.
  3. Leads a faculty meeting as soon as possible on the day of the death to explain events and procedures.
    a. Two meetings may be needed so that teachers can cover one another's classes.
    b. The faculty meeting may be held after school.
D. Students are notified.
  1. Individual teachers announce the death to their classes rather than using written notification.

    2. Teachers should offer a support system to students so that they may discuss their concerns.

E. School administrator or designee on crisis intervention team notifies parents of all students to explain the facts and any special arrangements to be made.

    1. Notice can be hand-carried by each student.

    2. Memo can be mailed to parents, though it will not arrive until the next day.

    3. Parents of students close to the trauma or students having a hard time with it should be called.

    4. If it is deemed necessary for a student to be dismissed from school, parents should be notified. The student should be picked up only by a parent or guardian.

F. School administrator or designee should be prepared to speak to the press, responding to press inquiries with a factual statement based on the immediate family's definition of the crisis and specifying what is being done in the school.

G. The crisis intervention team meets at the end of the day to review what has been done and what still needs to be done.

    1. Reviews information dissemination.

       a. Was everyone notified, and how was news received?

       b. Is it necessary to update anyone? Parent letters can be written and mailed; an update memo can be provided to staff, who can read it to students the next day; a faculty meeting can be held after school to review progress.

c. Were school administrator and all team members updated as described earlier?

        d. What was reported to the press, if anything, and how was the press handled?

    2. Reviews adequacy of support services.

    3. Reviews likely sequence of activity for those most affected by the crisis.

    4. Reviews procedure for moving forward for students and faculty.

II. Assist in the Grieving Process

  A. Grieving is appropriate for both students and staff, and everyone should be allowed to show their grief. (Note that it is appropriate to not grieve.)

    1. Grief may come out as sadness, but anger must also be recognized as a part of the grieving process.

    2. Close friends and enemies are most vulnerable when someone dies and should be seen in separate groups as determined by the crisis intervention team. (Worst enemies are at risk because of guilt and thinking, "I caused it.")

    3. Teachers need to be sensitive to their students' need to grieve and should encourage students to participate in the programs noted in "B," below.

  B. Grieving can be done in the following ways:

    1. Group sessions in the classroom or elsewhere.

        a. Groups may be open to anyone who needs and/or requests such sessions.

        b. Specific groups may be brought together, such as close friends, enemies, and teachers who worked closely with the person who died.

2. Classroom discussions led by the teacher or a support team member, at the teacher's request.

3. Individual counseling:
   a. By the social worker.
   b. By the psychologist.
   c. By the guidance counselor.

C. The student's belongings and school items, in the event of a student's death must be dealt with.

1. Personal belongings should be returned to the family in an appropriate manner.

2. What to do with school items, such as the student's desk, can be discussed with the class (e.g., remove it, leave it empty, etc.).

III. **Explain School Policy for Commemorating the Death**

A. Funerals:

1. School will not be closed for a student's funeral. However, the school will:
   a. Provide support.
   b. Help keep individuals from feeling isolated.
   c. Clarify misinformation.

2. School may be closed for a faculty member's funeral.

3. Students who go to the funeral of another student or a staff member should be accompanied by an adult.

4. Experiences may be shared the next day, if needed, in class or with support services.

B. Suicides:

1. The school approach is to commemorate all lives that are cut short.

2. The school's emphasis should *not* be on glorifying the act but on discussing what can be done to prevent such acts in the future; a suicide should be viewed as a teachable moment.
3. The victim should not be eulogized.
4. The school schedule should be maintained as much as possible.
5. If the suicide occurs at school, the police should be called immediately and students should be kept away from that area of the building.

IV. **Help Students and Staff to Move Forward**
   A. Students and faculty need to know that it is appropriate to go on with the business at hand even though they are still grieving and to know that laughter and fun are appropriate.
   B. For adolescents, grieving may be a prolonged process, sometimes lasting throughout adolescence.
      1. Students having a particularly hard time can be referred for counseling.
      2. Students who are struggling at times but are able to function may require some understanding from time to time.
   C. The crisis intervention team should meet to evaluate the situation and the effectiveness of the actions taken.

V. **Points to Remember**
   A. Paradoxically, through a crisis such as death can come a closer, more caring, supportive school community.
      1. Administrators and faculty can be seen in a more caring, supportive, human role.

2. Community relations can improve as a result of outreach to parents.
   B. Numerous teaching points can be made during this period of time, for example:
      1. How such a crisis may be prevented.
      2. How to deal effectively, on a personal level, with a crisis.
      3. How to handle crisis situations.
   C. All staff, including teachers, administrators, and support team members should make note of students or staff who may require follow-up services and report their names to the school counselor or a member of the crisis intervention team.

What to Do When a Student Makes a Suicide Threat

The July 22, 1996, issue of *Newsweek* featured an article entitled "Suicide's Shadow" (Gleck, 1996), which relayed the story of two young female students from California who committed suicide just before graduating from ninth grade. Earlier in the school year, another student from the same school committed suicide. The events reminded the community of how dangerous the teenage years have become. The article included recent figures compiled by the Centers for Disease Control that show that teen suicide rates are rising steadily. Between 1980 and 1993, suicide rates rose 120% for 10- to 14-year-olds and 30% for 15- to 19-year-olds.

Some of the increase, as Liotta (1996) contended, is attributable to the fact that more students are depressed today than were in the past. Liotta listed a number of signs that may indicate the presence of depression in teenagers—and should be warning signs for parents and educators. These include lack of interest or pleasure, irritability, behavioral changes, loss of weight, change in eating habits, feelings of guilt, lack of energy, difficulty concentrating, low self-esteem, decline in schoolwork, sense of helplessness, sadness, sense of hopelessness, change in sleep patterns, restlessness, death-related thoughts, and suicidal thoughts.

With today's high rates of childhood depression, and increasing rates of teen suicide, one of the most common questions asked of us is what to do when a student makes a suicide threat at school. In our work with many students with serious emotional and behavioral problems, we have had to respond to such situations many times. We follow the guidelines set forth for educators by Guetzloe (1989), who made the following points about youth suicide and its prevention.

1. Never take a student's suicide threats or gestures casually. Do something, mobilize. A suicidal person may interpret any disregard of his or her suicidal signals as a covert wish that he or she should carry out the threat.

2. Do not be afraid to bring up the subject of suicide. The discussion will not encourage the student to go through with his or her plans; on the contrary, it will help the student to know that someone cares. By talking honestly with the student, you may save his or her life.

3. Question the student closely and carefully about a possible suicide plan. Ask: "Are you planning to hurt yourself?" "Do you have a gun (or pills)?" "When do you plan to do this?"

4. Do not debate the morality of suicide with the stu-

dent. Do not preach. The suicidal person is not thinking about morality but about an unbearable emotional stress.

5. Through discussion with the student, identify the major stresses or events that precipitated the suicidal behavior. Do not pretend to understand when you are unsure about the student's feelings.

6. Do not respond to what the student says with such statements as, "You have so much to live for," or "Think of all the things you have that others don't." Such statements may make the student believe that his or her thoughts are ridiculous.

7. Encourage the student to make use of other supports, such as parents, friends, a minister, school personnel, neighbors, and the mental health clinic. Let the student know that you will help him or her make contacts with those supports.

8. If the problem was precipitated by the loss of a romantic relationship, do not make such comments as, "There are lots of fish in the sea," and do not pass judgment. The loss of love may feel like the end of the world to a teenager.

9. Never leave a suicidal student alone. Stay with the student.

10. Remove anything from the immediate environment that the student could use as a weapon, and remind the student's parents to do the same.

11. Mention school and community events that will occur later in the day, week, month, and so forth. Try to get a commitment from the student to attend or participate in those events.

12. Be aware of the student's responses to you. If the responses are accepting and the student's mood im-

proves, continue with your present tactic. If, however, the student says, "Leave me alone!" respond with such statements as "I care about you," "I want to help you," and "I'll be here for you."

13. Be sure that the student has the telephone number of a crisis hotline or a counseling service.

14. Do not promise the student that you will keep his or her suicidal behavior secret. It must be reported to parents and a counseling center.

15. Try to get a commitment from the student to not hurt himself or herself and to call for help if he or she feels any kind of suicidal impulse again. You may want to write a contract with the student to get the student's commitment in writing.

16. Involve others in the school who may be able to provide support to the student. Other school personnel may assist in contacting the parents and the counseling service. Other staff may also be able to provide needed information about what is going on in the student's life.

17. Document all actions taken.

Specific Procedures for Suicide Threat Situations in Schools

We strongly recommend that all schools have in place specific procedures for dealing with suicide threats. Sample procedures that educators can adopt, or adapt, follow.

For all staff:

1. Take any suicide threat seriously.
2. Do not leave the student alone.

3. Remove anything from the immediate environment that could be harmful to the student.
4. Immediately inform the school social worker and administrator.

For the school social worker:

1. Talk to the student privately to assess the seriousness of the threat.
2. During all discussions, be supportive and encouraging; use active listening.
3. Do not hesitate to involve other significant staff members in developing an action plan for the student.
4. Keep the student's teacher(s) and the school administrator informed of what steps are being taken.
5. Call the local mental health center for consultation if needed. However, do not mention the student's name at this point.
6. If the student is under age 18, notify his or her parent or guardian and ask the parent to come in and sign a written release so that the local mental health agency can be contacted.
7. If the student is 18 years old or older and is her or his own guardian, discuss all plans with the student and obtain his or her permission to release information to others (by having the student sign a release of information form), including the student's parents and any other relatives with whom the student is living. If the threat of suicide is perceived to be imminent and the student is uncooperative, however, the student's signature is not needed: The parent should then be contacted immediately.

8. If the student's parent or guardian is willing to take the student to the local crisis evaluation site, offer to help in making the arrangements. Emphasize the need for immediate help if that is perceived to be the situation. Coordinate a plan of action with the local mental health center.

9. If the student's parent or guardian is unavailable and the threat of suicide is perceived to be imminent, seek the help of any significant other adult in the student's life, such as a relative, friend, minister, or doctor, and emphasize the need for immediate help. If any of these people are willing to help, offer to assist in making arrangements for transporting the student to the local crisis evaluation site. Coordinate this with the local mental health center.

10. If the student's parent or guardian or other significant adult is unwilling to help and the need for help is judged to be immediate, call the Children and Family Services hotline to report the neglect and to seek assistance. If necessary, call the local police for assistance in transporting the student to the local crisis evaluation site. Coordinate this with the local mental health center.

11. If the action specified in #9 or #10 is taken, a school staff member should accompany the student to the crisis evaluation site or meet the student there. If the student's parent or guardian does not arrive within a reasonable period of time, the staff member should contact the Children and Family Services hotline to report the neglect and to seek assistance.

12. Document the incident on a suicide threat record form. (A sample form is provided in Appendix G.)

*R*eferences

Gleck, E. (1996, July 22). Suicide's shadow. *Newsweek,* pp. 40–42.

Guetzloe, E. (1989). *Youth suicide: What the educator should know.* Reston, VA: Council for Exceptional Children.

Jay, B. (1989). Managing a crisis in the school—tips for principals. *National Association of Secondary School Principals Bulletin, 73*(513), 14, 16–18.

Liotta, A. (1996). *When students grieve: A guide to bereavement in the schools.* Horsham, PA: LRP Publications.

St. John, W. (1986, October). How to develop an effective school communications crisis plan. *National Association of Secondary School Principals: Tips for Principals.* An occasional publication of the National Association of Secondary School Principals, 1904 Association Drive, Reston, Virginia 22091, 1–2.

Watson, R., Poda, J., Miller, C., Rice, E., & West, G. (1990). *Containing crisis: A guide to managing school emergencies.* Bloomington, IN: National Educational Service.

SCHOOL SECURITY

*I*n this chapter we provide practical tips for dealing with the following school security issues: weapons in the schools, bomb threats, visitors, and hostage situations. We hope that all schools will put procedures in place for dealing with crises in these areas, for they may occur in any school. To assist educators, we have included in this chapter, as elsewhere, sample procedures that schools can adopt or adapt.

*W*eapons in Schools

J. Portner (1995) writes that a 1995 report issued by the U.S. Department of Justice stated that the number of teenagers arrested for weapons offenses—carrying or selling guns, explosives, or some types of knives—had more than doubled since 1985. According to the report, the increase in the number of juveniles arrested for gun possession reflected a larger trend of increased youth involvement in violent crimes.

Reports of student involvement in violent crime are all too common. Schools in cities and small towns, in rural and urban areas, have been affected. The following is just one of many such incidents. The Associated Press reported that on October 12, 1995, a suspended student walked through a back door at Blackville-Hilda High School in Blackville, South Carolina, armed with a revolver. He passed by two classrooms and entered a third, where he fired the gun at a math teacher. He then continued down the hall, where he confronted another math teacher, whom he shot to death.

With the increase in juvenile possession of weapons, schools must be prepared for incidents in which students confront school staff or other students with a weapon. Specific procedures must be in place. The following are our suggestions for what a teacher or other member of the school staff should do if he or she observes a student pointing a gun or other dangerous weapon at someone else in school.

1. Concentrate on staying calm. Instruct everyone not directly involved in the incident to leave the area. Another staff member should press an alarm button or immediately call the police from the nearest phone.
2. Stand a short distance from the student. Rather than directly facing the student, stand at an angle to the student's side. Use a nonconfrontational stance.
3. Focus on the student; avoid looking at the weapon.
4. Using a quiet and calm voice, attempt to negotiate with the student. Ask the student questions such as whether you can move back three steps. The more "yes"es you are able to get, the higher the chance that the student will not use the weapon. Further, the questioning will help you buy time until the police arrive. Again, the longer you can talk calmly

to the student, the less likely it is that the student will use the weapon.

5. Do not attempt to disarm the student unless you believe that doing so is the *only* way to prevent the student from using the weapon.

6. When the police arrive, follow their directions.

It is illegal for a student to carry a gun, concealed or in the open, at school. If a teacher or other member of the school staff has reasonable cause (see Chapter 8) to suspect that a student has a gun or other weapon in his or her possession at school, we recommend the following procedures.

1. Follow the school's search procedures (see Chapter 8). The search should be conducted by a team of school staff in an area that is away from other students but offers access to emergency exits, a phone, or both.

2. Should the staff conducting the search feel that the student is dangerous or threatening and in possible possession of a gun, the designated school officials should notify local police immediately.

3. Should a student suspected of having a concealed weapon refuse the search, the search team should explain to the student that, due to the perceived dangerousness of the situation, the police will be called if the student fails to comply with the staff search.

4. In the event that a weapon is confiscated during a search, school officials should notify the police and the student's parents. School officials should also call the police if a search reveals a questionable item (such as bullets) and request direction

on how the school should proceed. Whenever a weapon is found, the law enforcement procedures for the illegal action should be invoked.

5. All searches should be documented by the individuals involved in the search. The student's behavior during the search, the reasonable cause for the search, the staff involvement, parent notification, and search results should be included in the documentation. In the case that a crime was committed, the documentation should be sent to the officer in charge of the case, to the local probation office, and to the assistant state's attorney.

6. In the case that a search reveals a student to be in possession of a knife, it is up to the school to determine whether the police should be involved. It is not a crime for a student to carry a pocketknife in school; a switchblade, however, is considered a weapon and its possession in school is illegal. We believe that it should be against school rules to carry *any* type of knife at school or at school events. We recommend that school staff confiscate any knife that is found and render consequences as specified in school policy.

Procedures for Handling Bomb Threats, Bombs Found, and Bomb Explosions in Schools

In any public institution, including schools, the possibility of a bomb threat always exists. In the author's small city (with a population of 20,000), the local police respond to several bomb threats every year. While it is true that the vast majority of bomb threats are false, they never should be ignored. A sound procedure for handling this type of threat is imperative.

In the Event of a Bomb Threat

In the event of a bomb threat at school, the following steps should be taken:

1. The school principal should immediately notify the local police and all necessary staff.
2. The police and the school principal should evaluate the seriousness of the threat based on the following:
   - Is there a sign of illegal entry into the school?
   - Has there been a report of missing chemicals from the Chemistry lab or elsewhere in the school?
   - Have other recent bomb threats proven to be hoaxes?
   - Is it a day that students may not want to be in school, such as the first day of spring?
   - Was there giggling in the background when the bomb threat call was made?
   - Has there been a recent pattern of student, parent, or staff unrest?
   - Which students have been reported absent on the day of the threat?
3. The police and school principal should conduct a search of the building.

In the Event that a Bomb Is Found

In the event that a bomb is found in the school, the following steps should be taken:

1. The area in which the bomb is found should be sealed off while the police remove the suspected device.
2. The school should be evacuated in stages starting with those rooms nearest the device.
3. School officials should instruct students and staff to reenter the building after being so advised by the police.

In the Event of a Bomb Explosion

In the event of a bomb explosion while staff or staff and students are in the school building, the following steps should be taken:

1. One of the alarm buttons to the police department should be pressed immediately, and the fire alarm should be activated.
2. If the phones in the school are still working, the fire department should be notified. If the phones are not working, the police should be asked to notify the fire department.
3. The building should be immediately evacuated and every effort should be taken to keep students calm. School officials should instruct students and staff to reenter the building only after being so advised by the police and the fire department.
4. School officials should develop a list of casualties.
5. School officials should notify the school attorney.
6. An information center, staffed by school officials, should be set up to handle all inquiries about injured persons and the status of the school.
7. If the decision is made to close the school for the rest of the day or longer, transportation should be

arranged by school officials to get the students home.

8. School officials should fully document the incident. (A sample bomb threat report is provided in Appendix H.)

Procedures for Handling School Visitors

Visitor control is perhaps one of the areas of school security that is most often overlooked. The authors have noticed that we are almost never challenged when we visit a school. Many schools simply ignore persons who are walking the hallways and have no procedure in place for visitor control. Schools are public-supported institutions and belong to the community. It is difficult to develop a mindset that the community should not necessarily be allowed free access to all school areas. The safety of children and staff must be balanced against the public expectation of free admittance to community schools. Visitor control is a means to accomplish this task.

The format we have used in the following sample is one that is common to many school handbooks.

Purpose: The school believes in maintaining a safe environment for students and staff at all times. To maintain safety and promote the orderly functioning of the educational environment, the school requires that all visitors adhere to the following procedures:

1. All visitors will use the administrative entrance to the building.
    1.1 Signs will be posted to indicate the appropriate entrance.

2. All visitors will check in with a secretary.
   2.1 Visitors will notify a secretary of their business with the school.
   2.2 Visitors will sign in and sign out on a visitor register. (A sample page from a visitor register is provided in Appendix H.)
   2.3 Visitors will wait in the designated visitor waiting area while the secretary notifies the staff of their arrival.
3. Visitors will be given a visitor badge for use on the day of their visit.
   3.1 The visitor is to wear the badge at all times while in the school.
   3.2 A visitor who is seen not wearing his or her badge will be asked to wear the badge or leave the school.
   3.3 The visitor will return the badge to the secretary at the end of the visit.
4. Visitors will be escorted or directed to their destination by the secretary or school personnel.
5. All visits to the school, a classroom, or staff should be prearranged with school personnel.
   5.1 Visits during school hours should be for legitimate school business purposes.
   5.2 Classroom visits or observations should be prearranged with the classroom teacher, his or her supervisor, or another designated individual.
   5.3 Visitors who wish to monitor a classroom via an observation room must have permission from the teacher or his or her supervisor.
6. Students will be given an explanation of the school's expectations and procedures concerning visitors.

6.1 At the beginning of the school year, teachers will explain the visitor procedures to their students.

6.2 Students will be given directions (as specified herein) about what to do if they see a visitor in the school who is not wearing a visitor badge.

    a. Students will, calmly and quietly, immediately report the presence of the visitor to the nearest staff member.

    b. Students will not confront the visitor.

7. Staff will adhere to the following procedures with regard to school visitors.

7.1 All staff will review the school's visitor procedures with their supervisors at the beginning of the school year.

7.2 Staff will be aware of visitors and check to be sure that they are wearing their badges.

7.3 In the event that a visitor is seen not wearing his or her visitor badge, the following procedures will be followed:

    a. Two to three staff members will, together, approach the visitor and ask him or her to walk with them to the visitor entrance, where they are to obtain a visitor badge and sign in.

    b. Should the visitor resist complying with the school procedures, one staff member should quietly leave the area to notify the school administrator and the police, if he or she feels that police involvement is needed. (That staff member will let the others know his or her intent by using a prearranged hand signal.)

    c. In the event that a visitor who resists complying with school rules is unruly or appears to be potentially dangerous, one staff member should immediately notify the police department for assistance. (Again, the staff member will use a prearranged hand signal to alert the other staff of his or her intent.) When talking to the police, the staff member will clearly state that the safety of the students may be at stake.

d. The staff members who did not leave to notify the authorities should remain in the proximity of the visitor/intruder. The staff member who made the initial contact with the visitor/intruder should continue to talk to the intruder, if possible, to gain his or her compliance with the school procedures. The staff member who left to notify the authorities will, after doing so, alert all classroom teachers through a coded message over the intercom system to have everyone remain in the classrooms. (The code will be determined by staff at the beginning of the school year.) Teachers and staff in the classrooms will close and lock the classroom doors when this code is given.

e. Whenever a situation of visitor noncompliance arises, the staff members who intervened should, immediately after the incident, file a written summary of the incident with the school principal. (A sample noncompliant school visitor report is included in Appendix H.) A copy of the report should be placed in an appropriate file.

Procedures for Dealing with Hostage Situations in Schools

For the purposes of this discussion, we define a hostage situation as a situation in which one individual or a group of individuals prevents, through the use of verbal threats, intimidation, force, threats with weapons, or other means, another individual or group of individuals in a school from moving freely. In the event that an individual or group of individuals places students or staff in a hostage situation at school, we recommend that the following procedures be followed. The purpose of these procedures, as of all other procedures in this book, is to maintain the safety of all students and staff.

1. One entrance to the school will be designated as the official entrance into the building. A secretary will be stationed close to that entrance to check in visitors. All visitors shall check in with the secretary, who will explain the school procedures for visitors. All entrances other than the official entrance shall be locked, so that no one may enter through them during the school day.

2. An emergency alarm system shall be established whereby alarm buttons, directly connected to the local police station, will be strategically placed in the school. The alarms are to be used only in the following situations: a hostage situation, a situation in which an individual is brandishing a weapon with the intent to harm, and other situations that present clear and imminent danger to students, staff, or both, that cannot be managed without outside

assistance. The alarm buttons shall be pressed only by school-designated officials.

3. A hand signal, which shall be determined by staff at the beginning of the school year, shall be used to indicate the need for someone to press an emergency alarm button. The signal shall also be used to indicate the need for further action, such as clearing the building.

4. In the event of a hostage situation in which a weapon is involved, all students and staff who are not hostages will be evacuated, to the preestablished location including everyone in the administrative wing. The evacuation procedure will be the same as that established for fire drills with the exception that notification of the evacuation will be made by word of mouth rather than by audible alarm. The use of an alarm could escalate the hostage situation.

   Students and staff who are evacuating will reassemble at a preestablished meeting area some distance from the school building. They will be directed to stay away from any window area or area visible to the hostage taker.

   Teachers will be in charge of their students and will be responsible for keeping their classes occupied and calm.

   Law enforcement officials will assist in transporting students to the preestablished location.

5. The staff member(s) (administrator or designee) directly dealing with the hostage situation should handle it in the following manner:

   a. Remain calm. (Bear in mind that as long as everyone is alive, your efforts are working.)

Make every effort to keep everyone involved in the situation calm.

b. Refrain from making any deals with the hostage taker. Law enforcement officials should be the only individuals to negotiate with a hostage taker.

c. In the event that both students and staff are taken hostage, suggest that the hostage taker release the students.

d. Cooperate with the hostage taker.

e. Avoid trying to negotiate with the hostage taker other than to suggest the release of students.

f. Avoid questioning any law enforcement tactics or actions while students or staff are being held hostage.

g. Make every effort to keep the hostages from questioning law enforcement tactics.

h. Remain patient. Expect that resolving the hostage situation will take time.

i. Do not be alarmed if power is disconnected, food is not sent, or deadlines are missed. Such occurrences are not unusual in a hostage situation.

j. Realize that experts are working hard to effect the hostage release. All of their tactics and actions, even those that may appear to be unrelated to the hostage release, do have that purpose.

k. Know that law enforcement officials will act immediately if a violent act occurs. Should such an act occur, take cover, get away, and cooperate with any police command.

l. In the aftermath of a hostage situation, avoid discussing the situation until law enforcement officials have completely finished their investigation.

  m. Be aware that bonding and sympathizing syndromes may occur in a hostage situation.

  n. Remember to respect the confidentiality of students and possible items of evidentiary value if you are interviewed by the media.

6. All staff should receive in-service training at the beginning of each school year on the procedures and precautions set forth herein. During that training, the warning hand signal discussed previously shall be established. (We have used the following hand signal: The signaler puts one hand behind his or her back or out to the side and discretely extends one finger if the situation is manageable and no assistance is needed. If the situation is questionable and the signaler feels that he or she may need help, two fingers are extended to request assistance. If the signaler considers the situation dangerous, he or she extends three fingers to signal that another staff member should press the alarm button.)

References

Associated Press. (1995, October 13). Teacher, student killed in high school shooting. *Jacksonville (Illinois) Journal-Courier,* p. 7.

Portner, J. (1995, November 22). Juvenile weapons offenses double in decade, report says. *Education Week,* p. 3.

CONCLUSION

Our purpose in writing this book was to provide educators with guidelines for how to make their schools safe, hostile-free environments for all students and staff. In a recent Louis Harris and Associates survey (New York Times News Service, 1996) 1 in 9 students reported that they had cut class or stayed away from school because of the fear of crime. For students from high-crime neighborhoods, that figure rose to 1 in 3. The survey revealed that 20 violent deaths occurred in the schools in the 1994–1995 school year; in the first half of the 1995–1996 school year, there were 26 violent deaths according to the National School Safety Center, as reported by the New York Times News Service. Frank Newman, president of the Education Commission of the States, called the problem of youth violence a "real cancer" (New York Times News Service, 1996). Schools must do their part in curing this cancer, and one way to do so is for educators to make schools safe havens for all students and staff. We hope that schools will solicit the assistance of police departments and will work in unison to establish and cooperatively enact policies and procedures such as those detailed in this book to accomplish this critical goal.

References

New York Times News Service. (1996, March 3). Recent spate of shootings renews concern over violence in schools. *The (Springfield, Illinois) State Journal-Register,* p. 16.

APPENDIX A

Sample Procedural Statement for Peer Mediation Among School Staff

In accord with the Happy Days School belief that school and work should occur in a pleasant, harmonious environment, the following conflict resolution procedure is in place:

1. Trained mediators available for staff-to-staff conflict are...(A list of names would follow of staff who had volunteered and had been trained in conflict resolution techniques.)
2. Any staff member having a conflict with another staff member is encouraged to sit down and work out the conflict with the other individual.
3. If the two individuals are unable to resolve the conflict, either of the staff members may approach any of the mediators listed above and ask for conflict resolution.
4. The requested mediator will then approach the other staff member and tell him or her that conflict resolution has been requested. The mediator will ask the individual to participate in the conflict resolu-

tion session. If both parties agree to participate, a mutually acceptable time will be scheduled for the session.

5. If it is deemed appropriate by all parties, another mediator may be asked to join the session.

6. Conflict resolution using Schrumpf's (Schrumpf, Crawford, & Usadel, 1991) method will be used. All sessions are to be confidential.

References

Schrumpf, F., Crawford, D., & Usadel, H. (1991). *Peer mediation: Conflict resolution in the schools.* Champaign, IL: Research Press.

APPENDIX B

Sample Communication Network for Addressing Truancy

The Role of the School

1. Keep accurate records of student attendance.
2. Contact the homes of all truant students each day the students are absent and document the contact.
3. When a student's absences exceed 5% of the total school days, notify the parents in writing and notify the truant officer who will then initiate communication with the parent through a home visit.
4. Provide weekly attendance records on such truants to the truant officer.
5. Notify appropriate agencies involved with these truant students, such as the probation office and DCFS.

The Role of the Truant Officer

1. Investigate all cases of truancy or nonattendance at school that are reported by school officials.
2. When a student's absences exceed 10% of the total school days, provide written notice in person or by mail to the student's parents that the child must be in school.
3. If previous actions fail to resolve the issue, the truant officer shall request that a petition for court action be filed by the state's attorney.
4. If a court order has been disposed requiring a minor to attend school or participate in community service, regularly report to the court if the minor is a chronic or habitual truant.

The Role of the State's Attorney's Office

1. Review any requests for court action. Determine whether they meet the criteria for chronic truancy and whether supportive services have been found ineffective or refused.
2. When filing petitions for court action, request that an adjudicatory hearing be held within 10 days and acted upon within 30 days.

The Role of the Department of Children and Family Services

1. Support and encourage parent compliance with school attendance laws.
2. Through caseworkers, convince families involved with DCFS to report their children to the school if they refuse to attend school.
3. Provide the truant officer with any information the department has about students' whereabouts if they are truant.

The Role of the Local Police Department

1. Assist school personnel and truant officers in home visits made to follow up on truancy.
2. If a truant student is located in the community during school hours, transport him or her to school when possible.
3. When notified by the school district that a student has left the school premises without permission during the school day, attempt to locate the student and return him or her to the school.

The Role of the Probation Officer

1. Monitor and report chronic or habitual truants to the court. (In some states, juvenile probation officers are prohibited by legislation to monitor truant activities. In those states, when a student's at-

tendance at school is required by court order, the truant officer or designated school official will report truant activity to the court.)
2. Have school attendance written into intake supervision, court supervision, and probation orders.
3. When meeting with juveniles, stress the importance of school attendance and appropriate behavior in school.
4. Be a part of the support system for parents and school authorities.
5. Include school attendance records with social histories prepared for the court's consideration.

The Role of the Youth Attention Center

1. Provide parent education as well as advocacy and referral services for clients.
2. Inform clients of laws pertaining to juveniles, including truancy laws, laws about harboring a runaway, and curfew laws, as well as juvenile actions that will result in authoritative intervention.
3. Impress on parents their responsibility for keeping their children in compliance with the law.
4. Help the truant officer and probation officer prepare authoritative intervention petitions for submission to the state's attorney.
5. Help clients learn of educational opportunities and services within and beyond their community.

Alternatives to Suspension in Place at Jacksonville High School

I. Preventive Approach
  A. Teach students school discipline code
  B. Establish communication network for staff to efficiently communicate with each other throughout the building
  C. Teach staff classroom management skills
  D. Teach staff crisis intervention skills

II. Disciplinary Actions—Progressive Approach
  A. Teacher detentions
  B. Ninth-period detentions
  C. Behavioral probation
  D. Removal from class for period of time
  E. Behavioral/attendance contracting
  F. Agency referrals
  G. In-school suspensions/guidance referrals
  H. Alternative discipline—attitude adjustment
  I. Alternative discipline—school service project
  J. Reductions with parent conferences—negotiated; suspension days *could* be reduced if a parent conference held
  K. Initiate Parent Shadow Program—parent spends portion of a day following student to classes
  L. Extended in-school suspension
  M. Initiate Conflict Management Program
  N. Peer mediation
  O. Administrator/guidance mediation
  P. Administrator arbitration

III. Student Services
  A. Lifesavers—a student peer counseling group
  B. Leadership training

C. Peer mediation
D. Student Government
E. Special needs assessment
F. Student Alliance
G. Educational Support Program
H. Supportive Education Program

Source: John Bailey, Jacksonville High School (1994). Jacksonville, IL. Reprinted with permission.

Sample Truancy Ordinance

The following is the truancy ordinance that was implemented in the city of Jacksonville, Illinois.

Ordinance No. 94-0-19

AN ORDINANCE AMENDING CHAPTER 18, MISCELLANEOUS OFFENSES, PROVISIONS., OF THE MUNICIPAL CODE OF THE CITY OF JACKSONVILLE ILLINOIS (Re: add new Section 18-28, Truancy)

BE IT ORDAINED BY THE CITY COUNCIL OF THE CITY OF JACKSONVILLE, MORGAN COUNTY, ILLINOIS:

Section 1: That Chapter 18, Miscellaneous, Provisions., of the Municipal Code of the City of Jacksonville, Illinois, be amended by adding thereto the following language as new Section 18-28, Truancy:

"(A) Any person subject to compulsory school attendance under the Illinois School Code (105 ILSC 5/26), who is absent from such attendance without valid cause for all or any part of a school day, shall be deemed to be a truant and shall be in violation of this Section 18-28 (A).

(B) Any person having custody or control of any child subject to compulsory school attendance under the Illinois School Code, who knowingly and willfully permits such child to be absent from such attendance without valid cause for all or any part of a school day, shall be in violation of this Section 18-28 (B).

(C) As used in this Section 18-28, "valid cause" shall be illness, observance of a religious holiday, death in the immediate family, or family emergency, and shall include such other situations beyond the control of the student as determined by the Board of Education in each district, or such other circumstances which cause reasonable concern to the parent for the safety or health of the student.

(D) Any person violating the terms of Section 18-28 (A) or 18-28 (B) shall be subject to fine, upon conviction, of not less than Twenty-five Dollars ($25.00) and not more than One Hundred Dollars ($100.00): in addition to or in lieu of the penalties set forth herein, a period of community service not to exceed one hundred sixty (160) hours, and/or a requirement that the person attend Parent Assistance classes, may be imposed upon a person who violates any provision of this Section. Each day upon which a violation occurs shall constitute a separate offense."

Section 2: That all ordinances, parts of ordinances, and amendments to ordinances in conflict with any provision of this ordinance are repealed as of the effective date hereof.

Section 3: That the City Clerk is hereby instructed to publish this ordinance in Pamphlet Form.

Section 4: That this ordinance shall be in full force and effect from and after its passage, approval, and publication in Pamphlet Form as provided by law.

PASSED AND APPROVED at a regular meeting of the City Council of the City of Jacksonville, Illinois, this 25th day of April, 1994.

_____
Mayor

ATTEST:

_____
City Clerk

Note: From "An ordinance amending Chapter 18, Miscellaneous Offenses, provisions., of the Municipal Code of the City of Jacksonville, Illinois," by R. Tendick, 1994. Reprinted with permission.

Sample Agreement Between a City and a School District for Monitoring the Court-Ordered Community Service of Truant Students

This agreement made and entered into this 30th day of January, 1992, by and between the City of _____, hereinafter referred to as "City," and _____ School District, hereinafter referred to as "School," Witnesseth,

WHEREAS, School has requested that City adopt a Truancy Ordinance to combat the truancy problem in the School, and,

WHEREAS, a component of said Truancy Ordinance would be a community service program, whereby certain violators of the ordinance would be ordered to perform community service, and,

WHEREAS, the City is unable to administer said community service program, and School is willing to undertake the administration and operation of such community service program;

NOW THEREFORE, the parties agree as follows:

1. School hereby agrees to accept full and complete responsibility for the establishment, administration, and operation of a community service program in connection with any community service imposed by the Circuit Court of the _____ Judicial Circuit, _____ County, _____ State, as one punishment under the truancy ordinance adopted by the City.

2. School agrees to save, hold harmless, and indemnify City from any and all liability arising out of the establishment, operation and administration of the community service program.

3. School would adopt the policies and procedures for the establishment, operation, and administration of the community service program in substantially the form attached hereto as Exhibit "A"; School will promptly notify City of any changes in said policies and procedures.

This Agreement may be terminated by either City or School upon ninety (90) days' written notice, provided, however, that regardless of any termination hereunder, School would be responsible for completion of all work associated with any community service order imposed by the Court prior to the notice of termination.

This Agreement is entered into by the City pursuant to _____ Complied Statutes, Chapter _____, Paragraph _____, the Inter-Governmental Cooperation Act.

The City of _____

By _____

The School District of _____

By _____

EXHIBIT A: POLICIES AND PROCEDURES TO BE IMPLEMENTED BY THE SCHOOL DISTRICT

COMMUNITY SERVICE WORK PROGRAM

The purpose of this program is to provide the opportunity for completion of the community service condition ordered by the Court for violation of any truancy ordinance or resolution adopted by the city of _____.

The program shall be conducted at _____ School.

The operation of the program shall be the responsibility of an administrator of _____ School.

Supervision

Each student ordered to perform community service work shall be assigned to the caseload of _____ School. Each parent ordered to perform community service shall be assigned to the caseload of _____ School.

Assignment

Upon the Court ordering community service supervision, the student/parent/guardian shall report to the administrator; the administrator shall then determine the appropriate site and schedule with the student/parent/guardian and the student/parent/guardian shall sign a statement of understanding concerning the performance of community service work, which shall detail the community service work to be performed, the schedule for performance of said work, and the requirements for satisfactory completion of the community service.

Verification

The administrator shall document the hours worked and forward the information to the City Attorney. If the agreed schedule is not met, the administrator will notify the City Attorney.

Successful Completion of Work Conditions

Upon successful completion of the student/parent/ guardian's community service work conditions, the administrator shall complete a verification form and file it with the Court.

Failure to Complete Work Conditions

Should the administrator feel that the student/parent/guardian is not making a sincere effort to comply with the community service work conditions, the administrator shall consult with the City Attorney to determine the appropriate course of action.

References

Bailey, J. (1994). *Alternatives to suspension in place at Jacksonville High School.* (Available from John Bailey, Superintendent, Waverly Schools, Waverly, Illinois 62692.)

Tendick, R. (1994). An ordinance amending Chapter 18, Miscellaneous Offenses, provisions., of the Municipal Code of the City of Jacksonville, Illinois (Re: Add new Section 18–28, Truancy). Jacksonville, Illinois: City of Jacksonville.

APPENDIX C

Sample Police Incident Report

Student _____

File #_____ Date_____ Age_____ Date of Birth _____

Address_____

Parent/Guardian_____

Address_____

Victim_____

Age_____ Date of Birth_____

Adult Witness(es)—Name/Position _____

_____

_____

Date/Time of Incident _____

Location of Incident _____

Type of Incident_____

Injuries/Damage _____

Object of Incident (Assault, Theft, Etc.) _____

_____

Method (Hit with Fist, Threw Object, etc.)_____

Officer Involved _____

Narrative (Write exactly what student and victim said or did during the incident; give specific details of incident)

_____

_____

_____

_____

_____

_____

_____

_____

_____

_____

_____

Report Made by _____

Position_____

Date _____

School_____

School Address _____

Copy sent to: Police __; Probation __; State's Attorney __

Note: Adapted from *Techniques for Managing Verbally and Physically Aggressive Students* (p. 144), by B. Johns, & V. Carr, 1995, Denver: Love.

References

Johns, B., & Carr, V. (1995). *Techniques for managing verbally and physically aggressive students.* Denver: Love.

APPENDIX D

Sample Document Prepared for School Administrators and Teachers: Criminal Behavior Requiring Police Notification

If your school involves the police when criminal behavior occurs, guarantee that the school's use of police intervention is firm, fair, and consistent for all students.

The following are illegal activities in the schools in Illinois.

1. Carrying a beeper at school.
2. Criminal damage to school property that has a dollar value greater than a specified amount agreed upon with the local police. (Damage in any amount is technically a violation of law and could be prosecuted. Practicality and common sense dictate that the police are not going to be called for destruction of a twenty-five cent pencil. A dollar amount of damage should be jointly worked out between the police and school before the police are involved in a damage case.)
3. Assault with the intent to harm.
4. Possession of a weapon.
5. Possession of illegal drugs.
6. Sales of drugs or look-alike drugs on or within 1,000 feet of school property.
7. Significant theft of school property or the personal property of another.

APPENDIX E

Sample Procedural Statement for Conducting School Searches

Introduction

The administrator or his or her designee may properly conduct or authorize a search of a student at school or on the school bus when the purpose of that search is to maintain the safety and discipline of the student body or to promote the orderly functioning of the educational environment. Searches will be conducted only to obtain evidence of violations of law or school policies.

Written notification that searches will be conducted will be provided to the students at the beginning of the school year and notices to that effect will be posted in the school. Written notice will also be provided to parents and students prior to the beginning of the school year.

A. Reasonable Cause

Search of students will be conducted only when a staff member has reasonable suspicion of a law or school violation based on one or more of the following:

- Reliable reports or information from credible sources made known to school staff. If the source is anonymous, the information must show that the informant has a relationship to the school or student so as to give the information credibility.
- Suspicious or evasive behavior by a student suggesting the violation of a school policy or a law or the concealment of contraband, weapons, or stolen property.

- Observation of a student engaging in prohibited conduct or suspected prohibited conduct.
- Verbal statement by a student that he or she has in his or her possession a weapon or other contraband or intends to harm students or staff with a weapon.
- Suspicion that a student, during an unauthorized absence from school, went to a location where a weapon or other prohibited item would be available.

The school staff may also take into account a student's disciplinary history when ascertaining whether reasonable suspicion exists.

B. Reasonable Scope—Justifying the Procedure

The scope of the search conducted must be reasonable in relation to the objective sought and the evidence searched for. The search shall follow the step by step process outlined in the School Procedures section of this handbook. In determining if the search is related to the objectives sought, staff will consider:

- The nature and severity of the violation to determine the amount of intrusion into the student's privacy rights.
- The area to be searched so that it will not be more extensive than required to serve the school's legitimate objectives.
- The time and place where the search will be conducted so that it will be as close as possible to the time and location of the suspected violation.
- The duration of the search so that it is no longer than necessary to serve the school's legitimate objectives.

C. Locker and Desk Searches

Searches of lockers, desks, storage spaces, and other property owned jointly by the school or the home school district and the student may be conducted whenever reasonable suspicion exists that contraband, weapons, or prohibited items are concealed therein. Notice of the joint ownership of lockers and desks shall be given to students and parents at the beginning of each school year.

D. Searches of Students and Their Personal Belongings

A search of a student and his or her personal belongings will be conducted when there is reasonable cause and according to the procedures outlined elsewhere in the handbook.

E. Strip Searches

In the event that there is reasonable cause that a student may be in possession of contraband, weapons, or other prohibited items and that the item(s) are located on the student's person in an area that would require a strip search, school staff will immediately contact the police department to determine further action.

F. Metal Detectors

School staff shall search a student with a metal detector when a need has been demonstrated to protect students and school officials from having dangerous weapons brought into the school or onto a school bus. Notice of such a search will be given to the student prior to the search.

G. Surveillance

Surveillance shall be conducted only in hallways, classrooms, school buses, and other areas that are open to public view and accessible to students.

H. Random Sweeps

Random sweeps will be conducted only in cases of emergency where exigent circumstances require immediate action to avoid danger to persons or property.

I. Police Involvement

Police involvement shall be sought whenever school officials uncover evidence of a violation of state law or deem such involvement necessary or helpful in maintaining school or bus safety. The police standard for a search or seizure is probable cause.

J. Reports

After a valid search has been conducted, school officials will prepare a written report that details the objectives of the search, the scope of the search, and the circumstances and information causing reasonable suspicion for the search. Copies of the report shall be filed in the student's temporary record. School officials will provide parents with a copy of the report.

Sample Search and Seizure Report

Name of Student _____

File #_____

Date_____Time of Search _____

Person(s) Conducting the Search _____

_____

Witnesses _____

_____

Location of the Search _____

Description of the Search _____

_____

_____

_____

_____

_____

_____

Cooperation Level of the Student _____

_____

Reasonable Cause for the Search _____

_____

Objective of the Search _____

_____

_____

Items Found _____

Action Taken _____

_____

_____

_____

_____

Signature of Person
Completing Report

_____

Position

_____

Date

cc: Parents

APPENDIX F

Sample Sexual Harassment Policy

A. Philosophy

It is the philosophy of this school that our students will be provided with an educational environment free of unwelcome sexual advances, requests for sexual favors, and other verbal or physical conduct or communications constituting sexual harassment as defined in Title VII of the 1964 Civil Rights Act (42 USC 2000e et seq). It shall be a violation of school policy for any student or staff member to harass another student or staff member through conduct or communications of a sexual nature.

School officials shall be responsible for promoting to all students and staff an understanding and acceptance of, and assuring compliance with, state and federal laws and school procedures governing sexual harassment within the school and on transportation to and from school. Violations of these laws and procedures will be cause for disciplinary action and will constitute a major infraction.

B. Definition

Sexual harassment is defined as any unwelcome sexual advances or requests for sexual favors or any conduct of a sexual nature when:

1. Submission to such conduct is made, either explicitly or implicitly, a term or condition of an individual's status as a student,
2. Submission to or rejection of such conduct by an individual is used as the basis for decisions affecting such individual, or

3. Such conduct has the purpose or effect of substantially interfering with an individual's work or school performance or creating an intimidating, hostile, or offensive school environment.

This definition is in accord with that specified by the National Women's Law Center, which indicates that there are two types of sexual harassment: "Quid pro quo harassment involves the conditioning of a benefit on the offering of sexual favors. Hostile environment harassment involves the maintenance of an atmosphere which unreasonably interferes with an individual's performance and/or creates a hostile or offensive environment."

Sexually harassing behaviors can include but are not limited to:

- Sexual jokes, language, epithets, advances, or propositions
- Possession or display of sexually suggestive objects, pictures, magazines, or cartoons
- Comments about a person's body or sexual orientation, prowess, or deficiencies
- Touching, leering, whistling, or suggestive, insulting, or obscene comments or gestures
- Verbal harassment targeted consistently at only one sex, even if the content of the verbal abuse is not sexual

C. Procedures

Any person who alleges sexual harassment by a staff member or student at the school may complain directly to the principal or assistant principal, as may any third person with knowledge or belief of conduct that may constitute sexual harassment. Filing such a complaint will not reflect upon the individual's status, nor will it affect future employment, grades, or work assignments. The school official to whom the complaint was reported will, within 24 hours, investigate the complaint by speaking individually to each party and any witness of the incident.

The person alleging harassment will be asked to document the incident in writing, if he or she will do so. Whether the alleged victim provides written documentation or not, the school official shall document the report in writing within 24 hours. All written reports will be made on a sexual harassment incident report form.

If, after a thorough investigation of the incident, the school official determines that the complaint was unfounded, he or she shall inform the involved parties of that decision and any written record of the complaint shall be kept separate from the employee's personnel file or the student's file.

D. Sanctions

If, after a thorough investigation of an alleged sexual harassment incident, the school official determines that the complaint was founded, the following will occur:

- In the case of a staff member, a substantiated charge will immediately be reported to the district superintendent and disciplinary action, in accord with school district policy, will occur.
- In the case of a student, a substantiated charge will constitute a major infraction and the student will be subject to all consequences of a major infraction. Mediation will be required of both the student perpetrator and the student victim so that they may resolve their differences and prevent future occurrences. When it is deemed appropriate by school

officials, the victim of the harassment may be asked to write a letter to the harasser describing his or her feelings.

E. Appeal

If, after a thorough investigation of the incident, a party is not satisfied with the decision made by the school official, the party has the right to appeal in writing to a three-person panel consisting of the school superintendent, the principal or assistant principal (other than the official who rendered the original decision), and a teacher named by the superintendent or his or her designee. The dissatisfied party and all other involved parties shall have the right to a hearing by the panel. That hearing shall be held within five school days from the time the request for the appeal is filed.

After the hearing is held, a decision will be rendered by the panel. That decision will be documented on an appeal of sexual harassment incident form and distributed to the involved parties.

If the appeal panel determines that the complaint was unfounded, that decision shall be provided to the involved parties and any written record of that complaint shall be kept separate from the employee's personnel file or the student's file.

F. No Retaliation for Reporting

Retaliation includes but is not limited to any form of intimidation, reprisal, or harassment. Anyone who retaliates against an individual who reports sexual harassment will be disciplined. Anyone who retaliates against an individual who testifies, assists, or otherwise participates in an investigation, proceeding, or hearing relating to a complaint of sexual harassment will be disciplined.

G. Notification

Notice of this policy will be circulated and explained to all students. It will also be disseminated to parents. Training sessions on the school's procedure for handling sexual harassment cases and complaints and on the prevention of sexual harassment shall be held for teachers and students on an annual basis.

Sample Sexual Harassment Incident Report

Date of Complaint _____

Name of Complainant _____

Description of the incident, including the name(s) of parties accused, the names of any witnesses, the alleged actions that occurred, any relevant background facts and circumstances, and the date of the incident _____

_____
_____
_____
_____
_____

Details of the investigation, including the names of the parties interviewed and the dates of the interviews _____

_____
_____
_____
_____
_____

Findings _____

_____

_____

_____

_____

_____

Corrective measures taken, if the complaint is determined to be founded, including the dates of the measures and the results achieved _____

_____

_____

_____

_____

_____

Attach the signed, written statement made by the complainant, if available, and any other relevant written statements.

_____

Signature and Title of
School Official

_____

Date

Sample Sexual Harassment Incident Appeal Report

Date of Appeal _____

Name of Complainant _____

Basis for Appeal _____

Summary of action taken by the school official who rendered the original decision _____

_____

_____

_____

_____

Members of the appeal panel _____

_____

_____

_____

_____

Summary of the appeal hearing _____

_____

_____

_____

_____

_____

_____

Findings of the appeal panel_____

_____

_____

_____

_____

_____

Corrective measures taken, if complaint is determined to
be founded, including the dates of the measures and the
results achieved _____

_____

_____

_____

_____

Attach all documentation filed regarding this appeal.

_____

Signature and Title of
School Official

_____

Date

APPENDIX G

Sample Suicide Threat Record Form

Student_____ Date of Birth _____

Parent(s)/Guardian(s) _____

Home Phone_____ Work Phone _____

Address_____

Description of Incident Causing Concern _____

_____

_____

Additional Observations (Check all that are applicable):

☐ Depression

☐ Moodiness

☐ Withdrawn

☐ Sleeping in Class

☐ Negative Self-Statements

☐ Giving away Possessions

☐ Suspected Drug Abuse

☐ Sudden Change in Appearance, Attitude, Quality of Work, Eating Habits, Life Situation, or Concentration

☐ Other _____

Explanation of Observations: _____

_____

Date/Time Parent(s)/Guardian(s) Contacted_____
    Who Was Contacted?_____

Perceived Reaction of Parent(s)/Guardian(s) _____
_____

Other Sources of Help Contacted (Check and provide date):
    ☐ Local Mental Health Center
    ☐ Clergy
    ☐ Relative
    ☐ Friend
    ☐ Children and Family Services
    ☐ Other _____

Release of Information Form Signed by Parent(s)/Guardian(s)
or Student if 18?   Yes_____   No_____

Action Taken or to Be Taken by Parent(s)/Guardian(s) and
Other Sources of Help _____
_____
_____

Action Taken by School Personnel _____
_____
_____

Further Action to Be Taken by School Personnel _____
_____
_____

Form Completed by_____
Date/Time Report Is Being Made _____

APPENDIX H

Sample Bomb Threat Report

Name of Person to Whom Call Was Made _____

_____

Date and Time of Call _____

Exact Words of Caller _____

_____

_____

_____

_____

Person receiving call should have attempted to ask the following questions. Write below any answers received.

1. When is the bomb to explode? _____

2. Where is the bomb at this time? _____

_____

3. What kind of bomb is it? _____

_____

4. What does it look like? _____

_____

5. Why did you put the bomb in this building? ___

_____

6. Where are you calling from? _____

_____

Description of Caller's Voice:

___Male ___Female ___Young ___Middle-Aged
___Elderly

Tone of Voice of Caller:

___Serious ___Joking ___Giggling or Laughing
___Tense ___Sure of Self ___Unsure of Self

Did the caller speak with an accent?____ If so, please describe _____

Did you recognize the voice?____ If so, whose? _____

_____

Describe any background noises _____

_____

Time Caller Hung up_____
Thorough Description of Action Taken _____

_____

_____

_____

_____
Signed

_____
Position

_____
Date

Sample School Visitor Register

Date	Name	Agency/Address	Purpose	Time in/out

Sample Noncompliant School Visitor Report

Visitor _____

Visitor's Address _____

Date _____

Describe the situation, purpose of visit, cause for concern

_____

_____

_____

Staff Members Involved _____

_____

_____

_____

Action Taken by Staff _____

_____

_____

_____

Results of Action Taken _____

_____

_____

_____

_____

Signed

_____

Position

_____

Date

AUTHOR INDEX

SUBJECT INDEX